Cost-Benefit Analysis and Environmental Regulations: Politics, Ethics, and Methods

Board of Trustees

The Conservation Foundation is a nonprofit research and communications organization dedicated to encouraging human conduct to sustain and enrich life on earth. Since its founding in 1948, it has attempted to provide intellectual leadership in the cause of wise management of the earth's resources.

Cost-Benefit Analysis and Environmental Regulations: Politics, Ethics, and Methods

Edited by
Daniel Swartzman
Richard A. Liroff
Kevin G. Croke

The Conservation Foundation
1717 Massachusetts Avenue, N.W.
Washington, D.C. 20036

COST-BENEFIT ANALYSIS AND ENVIRONMENTAL
REGULATIONS: POLITICS, ETHICS, AND METHODS

Copyright© 1982 by The Conservation Foundation

Library of Congress Catalog Card Number: 81-67851

International Standard Book Number: 0-89164-066-5

Cover design by Dick Sisk, The Associates, Inc.

Typeset by RFI, McLean, Virginia.

Printed by Universal Lithographers, Cockeysville, Maryland

The Conservation Foundation
1717 Massachusetts Avenue, N.W.
Washington, D.C. 20036

Contents

PART III SOURCES OF THE CONTROVERSY

PART IV   CONCLUSION

8. Excerpts

9. Conclusion

FOREWORDS

Foreword I

As this book was being prepared for publication, the executive and legislative branches of the federal government were launching major new initiatives to bring better accounting of costs and benefits to federal regulation. In February 1981, President Reagan issued Executive Order 12291, ordering executive agencies to conduct regulatory analyses of new and existing regulations. The order has the effect of requiring agencies to conduct cost-benefit analyses for their major actions, under the careful scrutiny of the Office of Management and Budget. Senator Paul Laxalt of Nevada is promoting a companion measure in Congress. The senator's omnibus regulatory reform bill would extend these economic analysis requirements to such independent regulatory agencies as the Federal Trade Commission.

These and other regulatory reform proposals have been inspired by the widely shared sense that government regulation often is not as effective or as efficient as it might be, and that regulators are not as sensitive to the economic consequences of their actions as they ought to be. Certainly, there is much to be gained from more deliberate attention to the economic impacts of regulation. But we must take care that our penchant for placing a price tag on government action does not seriously damage the precautionary approach to environmental protection embodied in such important laws as the Clean Air Act and the Toxic Substances Control Act.

Since its founding in 1948, The Conservation Foundation has recognized the importance of a healthy social and economic climate to the achievement of conservation goals and has believed that public policies should be based on rigorous factual analysis and public understanding. Therefore, we were pleased when Frank Beal, director of the Illinois Institute of Natural Resources, approached us in mid-1979, inquiring whether we would cosponsor a meeting on the role of cost-benefit analysis in environmental regulation. We quickly agreed, sensing that it was necessary to take discussion of cost-benefit analysis beyond the rarified realm of theoretical economics to explore some of its broader political and ethical ramifications.

The title we suggested for the conference was "Cost-Benefit Analysis and Environmental Regulation—Does it Clear the Air or Muddy the Water?" Conservationists are all too familiar with the abuse of cost-benefit analysis in the planning of federal water projects and fear that in regulatory analyses, the diffuse, long-term, hard-to-quantify benefits of environmental programs may be given insufficient weight relative to industries' concentrated, short-term, readily measurable compliance costs. Yet we also recognize that in an age of expensive energy, high inflation, and growing awareness of the intermedia impacts of pollution control programs, greater attention must be given to the costs and benefits of environmental regulations, and cost-effective alternatives need to be explored.

By cosponsoring this conference with a state agency that has considerable experience in economic analysis, and by inviting speakers with contrasting views to explore the larger consequences of applying cost-benefit analysis to environmental regulations, we hoped to learn whether there might be a middle ground between those having great faith in cost-benefit analysis and those who regard it as a threat to environmental programs. We wanted to identify the strengths and limits of this technique, and explore ways to capture its advantages and compensate for its limitations.

The conference was full and informative, and many of those present urged us to disseminate the proceedings to a wider audience. We hope this volume will be useful to both public officials and concerned members of the conservation and the business communities, as they consider the merits and drawbacks of the new executive and legislative initiatives.

Initial funding for this project was provided by the Illinois Institute of Natural Resources. Additional funding was provided through the Foundation's Business and Environment Program, whose principal supporters have been the Andrew W. Mellon Foundation, the Richard King Mellon Foundation, the Rockefeller Brothers Fund, and the Ford Foundation. Funds from an unrestricted grant from the Shell Oil Companies Foundation also helped to support this project by contributing to printing and publishing costs.

Niels Herlevsen served as project manager for the Illinois Institute of Natural Resources, and Janet Fesler coordinated the conference proceedings. Conservation Foundation Executive Vice President Terry Davies helped plan the conference, and Beth Davis edited the final manuscript for publication. Administrative support was provided by Tony Brown, Lynnette Clemens, Debbie Johnson, and Zeny Scott, from The Conservation Foundation, and by Adrienne Baloun and Roxane Moretti from the Illinois Institute of Natural Resources. We are indebted to our conference speakers for their well-conceived presentations and to our conference audience for their probing questions.

William K. Reilly
President
The Conservation Foundation

Foreword II

There is an inherent difficulty in pursuing pollution control goals. Stated succinctly, while it is essential to protect human health and environmental quality, it is equally essential that the means chosen be efficient, affordable, and realistic.

To make the right choices, decision makers must have some way of evaluating both the benefits and costs of environmental standards and strategies. Such difficult tasks are not accomplished well in darkness.

As Director of the Illinois Institute of Natural Resources, a state agency responsible in part for developing reliable information on environmental matters, I believe the state of Illinois has discovered a way of illuminating the process of making environmental choices: the economic impact statement.

In 1975 the Illinois General Assembly amended the state's Environmental Protection Act to require that the Institute complete economic impact statements on all regulatory proposals presented to the Illinois Pollution Control Board.

This action established both the requirements of an economic impact statement and a procedural framework for its use; further, it forbade the Pollution Control Board to adopt any regulation without first holding public hearings on the Institute's statement.

The Institute has since completed more than 75 economic impact statements. The topics have varied widely, but each has pursued one overriding goal: the realization of informed decision making based on an assessment of the critical environmental and economic impacts involved.

Other states and the federal government have been watching Illinois' efforts closely. Recent trends suggest that the economic impact assessment will be widely adopted within the next decade. Massachusetts, Indiana, North Carolina, and Utah already have adopted or are considering the technique, and the federal government is studying the Illinois technique as a model for its proposed requirements.

But because the practice is comparatively new, it is still developing and not without its problems. We in Illinois feel an obligation both to participate in this development and to share our experiences with others.

Toward this end, the Institute cosponsored a conference on cost-benefit analysis with The Conservation Foundation in Chicago in October 1980. This document consists of papers prepared for that conference.

The presentations included here point out many areas of agreement and disagreement over the techniques and value of cost-benefit analysis. Such discussion is extremely productive and should be encouraged. The Institute intends to hold annual conferences on the matter, and I trust will contribute thereby to the further development of a useful tool in the effort to achieve environmental goals.

The process certainly is proving successful in Illinois. It has helped us to see more clearly that, while benefits do accrue to human health, the natural environment, recreation, industry, agriculture, and energy, these benefits are not obtained without some measure of economic cost and social sacrifices.

I believe the Institute has overcome many obstacles in the past several years, having supported original research in benefits assessment, decision analysis, and a detailed model of the state's economy. These steps have been necessary to maintain a uniform and consistent consideration of important issues.

The papers presented at the Institute/Conservation Foundation conference have helped us clarify our purposes and modify our procedures. We hope the reader also will be informed and enriched by them.

Frank Beal
Director
Illinois Institute of
Natural Resources

Part I
INTRODUCTION

1/OVERVIEW

Cost-Benefit Analysis in Environmental Regulation: Will it Clear the Air or Muddy the Water?

Richard A. Liroff

The question posed above was examined at a conference convened in Chicago in October 1980 by the Illinois Institute of Natural Resources and The Conservation Foundation. This inquiry is not easy to answer, although glib responses abound. People concerned about environmental policy must respond—but must do so thoughtfully and pragmatically. Many of the following essays indicate that cost-benefit analysis, carefully defined and cautiously used, can contribute to sound, cost-effective policy, without compromising environmental goals. But these papers also point out the problems and pitfalls that are endemic to cost-benefit analysis.

The old adage "counters can't think and thinkers can't count" disparages those who depend either too much or too little on numerical calculations. Perhaps it is time to modify the adage and to urge counters to think carefully and thinkers to count carefully. In developing environmental policies, quantitative analysis of costs and benefits should neither be relied on exclusively nor ignored completely. An appropriate balance must be struck between numerical analyses and qualitative judgments so that those making decisions are not victimized by quantification or, conversely, by a reluctance to quantify.

Those with great faith in numbers promote cost-benefit analysis and related formal decision protocols. They suggest that their use will "clear the air" by readily measuring the impacts of actions and facilitating rational choices. Persons wary of quantification argue against cost-benefit analysis, suggesting that for many environmental decisions, quantification depends on so many questionable assumptions and leaps of judgment that numerical results serve only to "muddy the water."

Debates on this issue too often are muddled by a failure to define the term "cost-benefit analysis." At one extreme, some use a narrow definition, referring to the calculation in dollar terms, premised on formal economic theory, of all gains and losses from an action. At the opposite extreme, some view cost-benefit analysis as a systematic cataloging of all the positive and negative consequences of an action. Somewhere in the middle are those who define the term as a technique that measures impacts in dollars or other quantified values and that also provides systematic recognition of unquantifiable values and significant qualitative impacts.

It should be noted that references to cost-benefit analysis are sometimes accompanied by allusions to both risk-benefit and cost-effectiveness analysis. Risk-benefit analysis compares benefits and risks, often in regard to controls on toxic substances. Risks and benefits are compared quantitatively, although not necessarily in monetized terms. Definitions of risk-benefit analysis, like definitions of cost-benefit analysis, vary among authors. In fact, cost-benefit analysis and risk-benefit analysis sometimes are used interchangeably.

Cost-benefit and risk-benefit analysis can be used to determine if action will be taken—if benefits outweigh costs or risks. In contrast, cost-effectiveness analysis assumes that action towards a predefined goal will be taken and then identifies the most inexpensive yet effective means of action.

Readers of this volume should keep in mind each contributor's implicit or explicit definition of cost-benefit analysis. Readers should query whether a particular argument is based on concerns associated solely with a narrow, highly quantified, and monetized cost-benefit analysis, or whether it extends to a more broadly defined concept of cost-benefit analysis. Is an argument against cost-benefit analysis protesting the use of cost-benefit ratios as rules for making decisions or is it also objecting to the use of this technique as one of several tools contributing to more informed decision making? Does an argument apply only to the use of cost-benefit analysis in a specific context, e.g., helping define the numerical level of an environmental standard, or does it apply comprehensively, from defining a numerical standard to setting priorities for regulatory action?

The call for more cost-benefit analysis in environmental regulation stems from several concerns. Some argue it is politically motivated, sought by vested economic interests wishing to avoid costly pollution controls. Others maintain that sound public health and environmental policy require more analysis of costs and benefits to assure that scarce public resources are used wisely and that the factors entering a decision are made explicit to the public. To assure a maximum return on investments in environmental controls, they argue, it is important that the costs and benefits of individual actions be weighed so that the ratio of costs and benefits is reasonably consistent across actions. In other words, it may be preferable to devote resources to actions having the highest cost-benefit ratios and to forego those with lower ratios. Still others see a requirement for the analysis of costs and benefits as a means of prodding agencies working under considerable time and resource constraints to devote more careful attention to regulatory alternatives and to make clear to the public the factors that led to the final decision.

One of the major problems with the current debate on cost-benefit analysis is that the proponents and opponents tend to talk past one another. Some proponents argue that the technique should be a rule by which environmental decisions are made. Some opponents argue that it is unethical to measure human lives or other regulatory benefits in monetary or quantitative terms, and that we "dirty our hands" by even considering use of the technique. The middle ground in the dispute is held by those who maintain that cost-benefit analysis has some valuable applications, provided it is used only as a tool to contribute information to a decision rather than as a rule in accordance with which a decision must be made. Needless to say, it has been quite difficult to have a meaningful discussion among those holding these disparate views.

The purpose of the Chicago conference was to enhance discussion of cost-benefit analysis in environmental regulation. Since those debating the usefulness of cost-benefit analysis often approach that subject from different perspectives, disciplines, and value systems, the conference sponsors hoped that discussion at the meeting would help identify potential areas of agreement and clarify the reasons for remaining disagreements. The Illinois Institute of Natural Resources (IINR) commissioned papers, and The Conservation Foundation staff compiled excerpts and abstracts from numerous published sources to familiarize attendees with some of the most incisive and provocative assessments available of cost-benefit analysis.

The conference also was intended to acquaint participants with the IINR's economic impact assessment program. Since 1976, IINR, a state agency, has been required by law to prepare economic impact analyses for all environmental regulations proposed for adoption by the Illinois Pollution Control Board. IINR has produced over 75 economic studies and has issued several handbooks describing methods for measuring economic impacts and environmental benefits. From these efforts, IINR staff and consultants have developed a valuable base of knowledge about the usefulness of cost-benefit analysis in environmental regulation. Since other states are considering economic impact assessment programs, it seemed timely to identify some of the principal lessons of the Illinois experience.

This volume, containing the essence of the conference presentations and discussions, has three principal sections. Part II describes economic impact assessment efforts in Illinois and at the federal level. Part III develops a conceptual framework for discussing the principal points of dispute regarding cost-benefit analysis. Part IV elaborates on the preceding material and reports the results of a survey on the use of cost-benefit analysis conducted at the close of the conference.

The first essay in Part II, by Kevin Croke and Niels Herlevsen, describes the Illinois program. The authors are primarily concerned with issues of institutional design and the "scoping" of economic analyses. They discuss which regulations might be analyzed (particularly when the range of choice among alternatives is circumscribed or preempted by federal regulation), when and by whom the regulations might be analyzed, and how and by whom the range of alternative regulatory options might be defined for analysis. Croke and Herlevsen identify some of the principal lessons of the Illinois program and proffer recommendations to those considering economic impact assessment programs for other states.

The second essay, by Richard A. Liroff, provides a brief overview of the principal requirements for cost-benefit analysis in federal environmental programs and reports on efforts by the Environmental Protection Agency (EPA) and others to examine the costs and benefits of environmental regulations. Liroff notes that EPA has been conducting many assessments of costs and benefits, on its own initiative, in response to congressional requirements, and in accordance with executive orders. However, EPA conducts little formal cost-benefit analysis. Liroff contends that analyses of costs and benefits can advance environmental quality goals by helping to shore up public confidence in environmental programs and the public's willingness to bear the costs of these programs. He also suggests, however, that those who are vociferous in calling for an analysis of costs and benefits of environmental regulations should be equally loud in calling for close economic scrutiny of federal programs that on balance may be environmentally harmful. Such programs include subsidies for synthetic fuels development and subsidies for development on barrier islands and other flood-prone areas. Liroff also observes that, if information from those with an economic stake in regulation is perceived as dominating economic evaluation processes, government regulatory decisions may lose some of their legitimacy. Developing more flexible, cost-sensitive regulations is one way of getting government "off the back" of those it regulates, but reform of the regulatory process must not land government in the pocket of the regulated.

Part III begins with Daniel Swartzman's description of the conceptual framework that guided the conference discussions. He opens with an imaginary dialogue indicating how proponents and opponents of cost-benefit analysis can talk past one another. Reflecting on this dialogue, Swartzman contends that the conversation might be more directed and fruitful if the opposing contentions were categorized logically and then used as a basis for discussion. Swartzman identifies three principal areas of contention or question: methods, politics, and ethics. The methodological question focuses on how, technically, cost-benefit analyses are performed, and where uncertainty and the potential for biased judgments and errors exist. The political question looks at how cost-benefit analysis techniques are integrated into political decision-making processes. The ethical question inquires, among other things, whether the values environmental laws attempt to protect are demeaned when policy judgments affecting these values are made in quantitative terms. Each of Swartzman's major questions is elaborated upon in the remaining papers in Part III.

In their essay on methodology, Arthur Hurter, George Tolley, and Robert Fabian suggest that comparisons of costs and benefits are inevitable in decision making. Efficient use of resources is the primary concern in such assessments. Distributional considerations—allocation of resources among income, age, ethnic, and geographic groups—are also important, but the principal basis of formal cost-benefit analysis is efficiency. Hurter, Tolley, and Fabian recognize that distributional criteria are necessary supplements to efficiency criteria in public-policy decisions. They also concede that the actual distribution of income within society may influence the outcomes of conventional cost-benefit analysis techniques. For example, the value of some good sought to be protected by environmental laws is sometimes measured by a person's willingness to pay for it. Willingness to pay may depend significantly on the person's total income, and so goods valued by the poor may seem to have less worth in a cost-benefit calculation than goods valued by the wealthy.

Hurter, Tolley, and Fabian list many potential sources of error in standard cost-benefit analyses. But they do not believe that the possibility for error inevitably leads to the conclusion that cost-benefit analysis is useless and should be abandoned. Rather, they ask for patience and for greater effort to eliminate or reduce sources of error and urge "reasoned interpretation" of analytical results. They accept as a "fact of life" that personal or institutional biases of an analyst can influence a calculation, and that this should serve as an "admonition" to interpret results critically.

Like Croke and Herlevsen, Hurter, Tolley, and Fabian ponder how cost-benefit analysis can be made most useful for decision makers. They discuss options for determining the number of alternatives to be assessed, the degree of detail in such assessments, the degree of precision possible in the analytical results, and the presentation to decision makers of the uncertainties and possible sources of error in the analyses.

Dr. Richard N.L. Andrews' essay focuses on the political dimensions of cost-benefit analysis, examining disputes over its use as an instrument of regulatory reform. He argues that a fundamental basis for disagreements is philosophical, pitting those who believe in government as an "economic optimizer" against those who see government as an "imposer of normative constraints." Economic optimizers believe the primary concern of government should be the efficient allocation of resources. The normative constraints school, in contrast, holds that government is much more than simply an efficient resource allocator. Efficiency may be but one of several values involved in a government decision; competing goals on which a higher value might be placed by the government include such concerns as health, safety, environmental quality, and national defense.

Andrews illustrates the significance of this philosophical conflict by examining several questions at issue in the current debate over the use of cost-benefit analysis as a regulatory reform. For example, should government regulations protect the most sensitive and most heavily exposed members of society, or merely the majority? This question pits society's concern and respect for its vulnerable individuals against the general comfort and wealth of the majority. It may be more economically efficient to protect only the majority, but many may believe that the especially vulnerable and sensitive members of society have a right to breathe air that is not hazardous to their health.

Andrews comments that the current pressure for use of cost-benefit analysis in environmental regulation is in part a sincere effort by some to improve government decision making. But he adds that it is also a political weapon for challenging the recent primacy of environment, health, safety, and other consumer values, and for attempting to substitute for these a greater emphasis on business and producer values. Noting that cost-benefit analysis has been misused in the past, Andrews observes that in new proposals for cost-benefit analysis, there appears to be little evidence of safeguards against continued abuse.

Andrews suggests that the National Environmental Policy Act (NEPA) provides what may be an exceptionally apt analogy for predicting the effects of using cost-benefit analysis as an instrument of regulatory reform. He compares NEPA and cost-benefit analysis in terms of their substantive intent and their procedures, and then discusses such issues as manipulability and visibility of analyses.

Andrews expects that cost-benefit analysis will stop some of the least justifiable government proposals; will make some regulations more cost-sensitive; will retard new regulatory initiatives; and will increase the power of the President and the Office of Management and Budget (OMB) relative to agencies and the Congress.

Andrews concludes that cost-benefit analysis is a useful instrument for some kinds of regulatory reform. But it is not a panacea, and it is costly to use. Properly applied it may improve some decisions; improperly used, however, it may subvert regulatory actions that should be taken to protect public health and welfare. He suggests that cost-benefit analysis should not be used as a political weapon beyond its own legitimate purposes, validity, or cost-effectiveness, and that those who are most knowledgeable about it should be more outspokenly intolerant of those who use it inaccurately or misleadingly.

The final essay in Part III of this volume is Steven Kelman's discussion of the ethics of cost-benefit analysis. Drawing on formal ethical theory, Kelman contends that there may be many instances when a certain decision may be "right" even though its measurable benefits do not outweigh its cost. Moreover, there are several important reasons for not placing dollar values on nonmarketed benefits and costs, beyond the technical difficulties of doing so. After elaborating on some of the technical difficulties, Kelman contends that putting dollar values on nonmarketed items may reduce their value. He cites examples from the language of daily life, e.g., "buying friendship" and "prostituting oneself," which reflect social notions that some items should not be priced. These items derive their value from the fact that they are priceless or not for sale; in fact their nonmarketability affirms their high value.

Part IV begins with excerpts from discussions at the conference that highlight some important issues addressed by the participants and concludes with a summary essay by Daniel Swartzman. Swartzman observes that those involved in the debate over cost-benefit analysis can continue to engage in rhetorical stalemate and political battle or, alternatively, they can engage in a potentially fruitful dialogue. He reports the results of a survey of conference participants, which identified agreements and disagreements among environmentalists, business representatives, consultants, and government employees.

After briefly summarizing the potential contributions of cost-benefit analysis, Swartzman lists questions that can help identify analyses' limitations. He also ponders whether or how agreements might be achieved on outstanding methodological, political, and ethical disputes. He suggests, for example, that while proponents of cost-benefit analysis must accept the ethical problems inherent in some of its applications, opponents must be willing to define the limits of ethical danger. Swartzman concludes by stressing the importance of constructive dialogue, commenting that "if we sit back and take shots at one another, real progress in solving our economic and environmental problems will be impossible."

As Swartzman suggests, much remains to be resolved in the debate over cost-benefit analysis. But the following precis of the strengths and limits of cost-benefit analysis, and the recommendations to decision makers based upon it, represents an effort by The Conservation Foundation to encourage movement away from the adversarial positions that all too many partisans have thus far adopted.

STRENGTHS

- Cost-benefit analysis (CBA) provides a framework for structuring information and considering trade-offs.
- CBA helps make strategic choices about program priorities.
- CBA helps weed out the least desirable alternatives.
- CBA can identify areas in which uncertainty is greatest and further research is desirable.
- CBA can increase explicitness in decisions (although some people prefer obscurity), and thereby elevate the level of public debate and the usefulness of public participation.
- CBA can enhance consistency among decisions.
- CBA can help assess the cumulative effects of regulations on groups, industries, future generations, geographic areas, and so forth.
- CBA can improve the credibility of government by showing how decisions are made and that they are rational.

LIMITS

- Traditional CBA focuses only on efficiency, but other factors e.g., administrability, distribution of impacts, promotion of technological innovation, may be of equal or greater importance in decisions.
- CBA does not adequately account for impacts on future generations due to difficulties in deriving a present dollar value for future costs and benefits.
- CBA may place too much emphasis on translating gains and losses into dollar terms.
- CBA usually accepts technology as given and cannot anticipate technological breakthroughs that reduce costs.
- CBA may lead to inequitable decisions because the distribution of costs and benefits is not considered.
- CBA may lead to shortsighted and undesirable decisions because larger considerations—the political viability of agencies, preservation of the democratic system, "irrational" but strongly held views of the public, etc.—are ignored.

- Highly technical analysis may make administrative decisions appear even more inaccessible to the public.
- Simple displays of numerical ratios of benefits to costs (e.g., 3.1:1) presented without a guide to assumptions and uncertainties may lend a false air of precision to estimates.
- CBA may be considered unethical by some.

LESSONS FOR DECISION MAKERS

- Do not use CBA as a rule by which decisions are made.
- Do not translate gains and losses into monetary equivalents when reliable prices are not available.
- Recognize the specific circumstances when analysis of costs and benefits should be given little or no weight in decisions because of nonefficiency considerations or methodological limitations.
- Explicitly recognize important nonquantifiable values and have them accompany quantified analyses through the decision process.
- Conduct sensitivity or other analyses that enable decision makers to see how the range of outcomes is affected by manipulating important assumptions.
- Do not use cost-benefit analysis in decisions without a full explanation of the limits of estimates and the range of uncertainty.
- Recognize that while the most significant limits of CBA involve the translation of health-related gains and losses into monetary terms, more cost-sensitive regulation can be developed without monetization of benefits.
- Account for existing procedures for assessing costs and benefits before mandating additional procedures on an across-the-board basis.
- Staff regulatory agencies sufficiently to assure careful analysis of cost and benefit estimates prepared by others.
- Assure timely public participation, with full disclosure of analyses and all their important assumptions.

- Do not automatically favor one program over another simply because one is more cost-effective than the other. Non-efficiency considerations may dictate that the less cost-effective program is socially preferable.

Part II
EXPERIENCE TO DATE

2/STATE EXPERIENCE

Environmental Cost-Benefit Analysis: The Illinois Experience

Kevin G. Croke
Niels B. Herlevsen

Most of the discussion on the use of cost-benefit analysis in assessing environmental regulations has been based on the analysis of federal rather than state regulations. This is to be expected since the economic effects of federal regulations are more significant than and have been subject to greater scrutiny than state regulations. Furthermore, states have not used cost-benefit analysis extensively in developing their environmental programs.

The problems of designing a state program to conduct cost-benefit analysis now need to be addressed for a number of reasons. Foremost among these is a growing interest by states in mandating such analyses prior to the implementation of local environmental regulations. Illinois, North Carolina, Utah, Indiana, and Alaska have either passed or proposed legislation regarding the mandating of economic assessments.

A second reason for examining the design of state programs is that the problems faced by states in devising effective economic assessment programs are frequently different from those faced by the federal agencies. The regulatory structure and requirements of local programs may differ considerably from federal requirements. State resources to support cost-benefit analyses normally will be far more limited than federal budgets. Sensitivity to local issues may influence a local regulatory agency's design of regulations far more than federal agencies are influenced. This local sensitivity can lead to a greater emphasis on the analysis of distributional effects. Finally, the breadth of options open to state environmental regulatory agencies frequently is limited by federal preemption of authority.

The application of such concepts as reasonable available control technology (RACT) and best available technology by the federal government has restricted the options open to state or local environmental programs. For these reasons, states interested in initiating a cost-benefit or economic assessment program cannot simply model their activities after federal efforts.

A third reason for examining the design of state programs relates to the fact that both the division of federal-state responsibilities and the discretion of states in devising their own environmental protection programs are changing. Although federal preemption of authority generally has increased over the past decade, there is reason to believe that this trend may reverse itself in the next decade. There is a growing feeling that decentralization of federal powers to states may produce programs more attuned to local needs and conditions. The benefits and costs resulting from environmental regulation certainly are strongly influenced by local conditions. Furthermore, the nature of pollution control strategies seems to be shifting from exclusively the mandating of control equipment to controls that affect local growth and development. For example, early regulatory efforts focused on ensuring the installation of automotive emission control devices to reduce carbon monoxide. For those areas that still cannot attain air quality standards, further measures must be taken. Some of these include altering urban transportation plans, changing local land use controls, and establishing or revising siting regulations. These measures are examples of the types of actions that traditionally have been a local or state concern. As states are brought increasingly into the process of developing environmental protection programs in the next decade, regulatory assessment procedures such as cost-benefit analysis will become more commonplace on the state level.

STATE ECONOMIC ASSESSMENT PROGRAMS

States have evaluated their environmental programs in a number of ways. H. Brickman outlines three types of state economic assessment activities:[1]

Analyses that attempt to affect the content of environmental impact statements. These efforts normally are initiated to improve a state environmental impact statement (EIS) process by requiring an economic impact assessment of the state action for which the EIS is being prepared. Such assessments will include a description of the costs and benefits resulting not only from the proposed action but also from viable alternatives.

Requirements that alter the rule-making process of governmental agencies. These programs seek to foster economic analysis by those state agencies with authority to promulgate environmental regulations. Some form of economic analysis is incorporated into a formal economic impact statement for every proposed agency action.

Efforts to promote more economic assessment in the legislative process. This type of program looks at the benefits and costs of legislative actions.

In assessing these three types of programs, H. Brickman notes that many of the states adopting such programs have not carried out extensive efforts in their implementation. Factors that have restricted implementation include: (1) a perception by agencies involved that the development of economic impact studies would be a large administrative burden, (2) a lack of dollar or human resources, and (3) the administrative complexity of interagency cooperation in evaluating programs.

THE ILLINOIS PROGRAM

This discussion of a state environmental cost-benefit program focuses on the Illinois experience in implementing the second type of program—that aimed at governmental rule-making agencies. For the past decade, by their interpretation of federal guidelines and rule-making capacity, rule-making agencies have had a more profound and pervasive impact on states' environmental protection programs than have EIS actions or even state environmental legislative action. Illinois had the first economic assessment program directed at rule-making agencies and has had by far the most experience in administering such a program.

The Illinois economic assessment program began as a result of a state legislative initiative. The Illinois General Assembly amended the state's Environmental Protection Act in 1975 to require that the Illinois Institute of Natural Resources carry out economic impact assessments for all proposals presented to the Illinois Pollution Control Board. The Illinois Institute of Natural Resources is the state agency whose purpose is to carry out analysis and research in support of Illinois' environmental and resource development programs. The Illinois Pollution Control Board is a regulatory body created to issue environmental standards and promulgate state environmental regulations.

In the 1975 amendments, economic impact assessments were defined as follows:[2]

Each economic impact study shall include, but not be limited to, the following:

a) An evaluation of the environmental cost and benefits of the rules and regulations to the people of the state of Illinois, including the health, welfare, and social costs and benefits;

b) An evaluation of the economic impact of the rules and regulations on the people of the state of Illinois, including, but not limited to the effects of said rules and regulations on the following:
   1) Cost of goods and services
   2) Availability of goods and services
   3) Availability of employment

c) An evaluation of the economic impact of the rules and regulations on Illinois agriculture, including, but not limited to, the following:
   1) Cost of food
   2) Availability of food
   3) Availability of employment

d) An evaluation of the economic impact of the rules and regulations on units of local government, including, but not limited to, the following:
   1) Effects on local taxes
   2) Effects on local services
   3) Effects on local community expansion

e) Evaluation of the economic impact of the rules and regulations on commerce and industry, including, but not limited to, the following:
   1) Effects on prices
   2) Effects on expansion of industry in Illinois
   3) Effects on the availability of adequate supplies of energy
   4) Effects on the attraction of new industry.

Ordinarily, a proposal to the Illinois Pollution Control Board originates from the Illinois Environmental Protection Agency, from a state industry, or from a private petition by a concerned group. (See Figure 1.) The Board holds a number of hearings on the technical merits raised by the proposal, as well as its economic impact. Based on this evidence, the Board can either promulgate or deny the original proposal or pass its own modified version of the proposal.

Format of Ecomomic Impact Studies

Illinois has attempted to standardize, to some extent, the structure

FIGURE 1

**Proposal Initiated
by**

Pollution Control Board (PCB)
Illinois Environmental Protection Agency
Illinois Institute of Natural Resources (IINR)
Citizen or Private Group

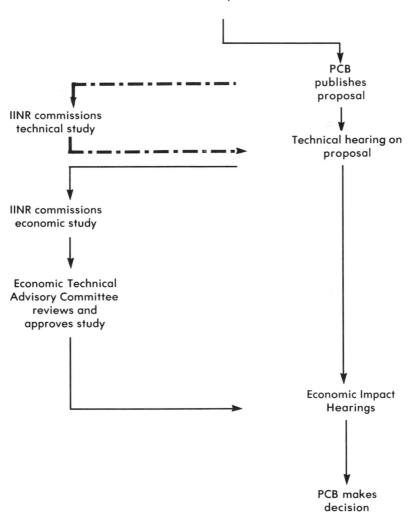

and format of its economic impact statements. A generic outline of an economic statement is presented in Table 1.

In the five years of its program, Illinois has prepared over 80 economic impact statements. Table 2 lists a sample of the type of proposals evaluated. For each study, major benefit and cost categories were defined and evaluated. Based upon information in these studies, Table 3 was developed to show the major categories of costs for each proposal, the bearer of such costs, and an estimate of the costs. Table 4 presents a parallel set of information for benefits.

TABLE 1

Outline of an Economic Impact Study

A. Motivation for the Regulation
    1. Rationale
    2. Major benefits derived
    3. Major cost categories
    4. Possible alternatives to the proposed regulation

B. Review of Current and Anticipated Environmental Consequences
    1. Review of environmental studies
    2. Presentation of state monitoring data
    3. Environmental modeling analysis

C. Benefit Assessment
    1. Identification of affected populations
    2. Description and estimations of environmental damages
    3. Valuation of benefits

D. Cost Analysis
    1. Identification of affected economic sectors
    2. Description of direct cost of regulation
    3. Estimation of costs
    4. Analysis of secondary economic impacts

E. Comparison of Benefits and Costs
    1. Discussion of magnitudes of relative benefits and costs
    2. Distribution of benefits and costs to different sectors
    3. Sensitivity analysis

SOURCE: Illinois Institute of Natural Resources. "Economic Impact Studies: Second Year in Review." Docket INR 78-18. February, 1979.

TABLE 2

Sample of Proposals Evaluated

AIR

Sulfur Dioxide Revisions	Proposed SO_2 emission standards for facilities outside of the Chicago, Peoria, and St. Louis major metropolitan areas
Sulfur Content of Fuel Oils	Would relax sulfur limitations of fuel oils used outside of Cook County
Air Furnace Emission Standards	Would relax particulate emission standards for an air furnace melting facility located in Hoopeston, Illinois
Low-Carbon Waste	Proposed change in particulate emission standards for incinerators which burn low-carbon waste

WATER

Polar, Non-polar Hexane Solubles	Proposal would change the allowable discharge of hexane extractable materials (HEM) for firms discharging both polar and non-polar HEM; would also change sampling methods
Mine Waste Dissolved Solids	Proposal to relax the total dissolved solids standard for coal mining operations
Feedlot Regulation Date Revision	Amendments to bring Illinois regulations into conformance with federal guidelines; of 10 proposed changes, only 2 may have substantive impact
Mercury Effluent	Proposal to relax the mercury effluent standard
Boron Exemption	Proposal by Illinois Power Company to exempt a short stretch of the Wood River and an unnamed tributary from the boron water quality standard
Selenium Effluent	Proposed deletion of the selenium effluent standard
pH Effluent	Proposal to modify pH effluent standards by narrowing the allowable range
Chromium Effluent	Amendment to tighten the effluent limitation for hexavalent chromium
Dissolved Iron	Would delete the total dissolved iron effluent standard
Ammonia Effluent	Regulation would exempt small dischargers from ammonia nitrogen standard and grant extensions for larger sources
Public Water Supplies	Proposal to bring Illinois into conformance with federal guidelines and qualify the state to assume primary enforcement responsibility for Federal Safe Drinking Water Act.

SOLID WASTE

Special Waste Hauling	Would establish a "cradle-to-grave" manifest system to allow accounting for movement of hazardous and other "special" wastes

SOURCE: Illinois Institute of Natural Resources. "Economic Impact Studies; Second Year in Review." Docket INR 78-18. February, 1979.

TABLE 3

Cost of Proposed Regulations

Regulation	Type of Cost	Who Bears Cost	Estimated Value
Sulfur dioxide revisions	Increase in control expenditures	18 large coal- and oil-burning utilities and industries	$15-16 million per year
Sulfur content of fuel oils	Deterioration of air quality and associated increase in damages	General public	$4 million in material damage (best estimate) plus nonquantifiable health effects
Air furnace emission standard	Deterioration of air quality and associated increase in damages	Residents in the vicinity of affected facility	$11,000 to $15,000 per year
Particulate standard for combustion of low-carbon waste	Deterioration of air quality and associated increase in damages	Residents in the vicinity of affected facility	$1,500 to $7,700 per year
Polar, non-polar hexane solubles	Increased levels of hexane-extractable materials in Illinois waters	Industrial water users and indigenous biota	Too small to quantify
Mine waste total dissolved solids	Increased volume of dissolved solids in streams receiving mine-related effluents	Residential and industrial water users	$163,000 per year plus nonquantifiable future impacts
Feedlot regulation date revision	Increase in control costs	Swine, dairy, and cattle farmers	Investment = $1,630,000; Annual operation and maintenance = $192,000
Mercury effluent standard	Increase in mercury levels in Illinois streams and associated increase in damages	Primarily aquatic life; also, human beings through biomagnification	Appears negligible — not quantified

Regulation	Type of Cost	Who Bears Cost	Estimated Value
Boron exemption	Increase in boron levels in a short stretch of stream	Certain aquatic species and crops	Too insignificant to quantify
Selenium effluent standard	Possible increase in selenium discharges	Water users	Negligible
pH effluent standard	Increase in control cost	Small municipalities and industrial dischargers	Between $250,000 and $760,000 annual cost, depending on final form of regulation
Chromium effluent standard	Increase in compliance cost	3 electroplaters and 4 other industrial dischargers	$4,500,000 per year
Dissolved iron effluent standard	Increase in dissolved iron concentrations in Illinois streams	Surface water users	Insignificant because other standards protect against excessive iron concentrations
Ammonia effluent revision	Deterioration of water quality for recreation and increase in chlorination costs	Surface water users, public water supplies, and some industries	$4.6 million per year plus nonquantifiable effects on biota
Public water supplies	Deterioration in aesthetic quality of some Illinois water supplies	Customers of public water supplies	Negligible
Special waste hauling	Administrative costs plus higher disposal costs	IEPA and special waste haulers	IEPA—$200,000 per year; Industry—$4,215,000 per year

SOURCE: Illinois Institute of Natural Resources. "Economic Impact Studies; Second Year in Review." Docket INR 78-18. February, 1979.

TABLE 4

Benefit of Proposed Regulations*

Regulation	Type of Benefit	Who Benefits Directly	Estimated Value
Sulfur dioxide revisions	Reduction in adverse health impacts and materials damage	Residents in the vicinity of affected facilities	$100,000
Sulfur content of fuel oils	Decrease in cost of desulfurization equipment	Petroleum refiners	$150 -$300 million per year
Air furnace emission standard	Savings in control cost, prevention of possible closure	An iron foundry in Hoopeston, Illinois	$32,000 per year or $13,000,000 total if shutdown
Particulate standard for combustion of low-carbon waste	Savings in control cost	Addressograph-Multigraph Corporation	$14,000-$137,000, depending on method utilized
Polar, non-polar hexane solubles	Reduced cost of treatment and pretreatment facilities	Industries in food processing, soap and detergent manufacture, leather production	Up to $12,000,000 if local ordinances are relaxed; $30,000-$110,000 per year if not
Mine waste total dissolved solids	Savings in controls costs	Coal mining industry	Up to $37,000,000 per year if standard is eliminated
Feedlot regulation date revision	Reduced damages from feedlot runoff	Recreation users of streams; also certain fish and fowl	Not quantified
Mercury effluent standard	Savings of control costs, avoidance of shutdown	Industry and municipal dischargers	$136,000,000 to $153,000,000 per year
Boron exemption	Savings in control cost	Illinois Power Co.	$33,600 per year
Change in selenium effluent standard	Possible savings in administrative costs; creation of "goodwill"	Industry and municipalities	Not quantified

Regulation	Type of Benefit	Who Benefits Directly	Estimated Value
Change in pH effluent standard	Increased protection for aquatic life; improved quality for recreation and industrial use	Primarily aquatic life	Not quantified but can be significant depending on levels of ammonia present
Change in chromium effluent standard	Protection of waters as future water supplies, and also for aquatic life	Users and aquatic life primarily in Cone and Aux Sable creeks	Not quantified
Change in dissolved iron effluent standard	Simplification of existing regulations	Industries discharging iron	Not quantified
Ammonia effluent revision	Savings in treatment cost	Municipal dischargers	Present value = $311 million; capital costs of $220 million plus annual savings of $21.5 million
Public water supplies	Qualifies state to assume primary enforcement responsibility for Safe Drinking Water Act; also savings in treatment cost	IEPA and public water supplies	$15.1 million per year
Special waste hauling	Reduction in level of uncontrolled dumping and associated damages	General public	$1,000,000 plus significant nonquantifiable reduction in risk

* In cases in which the proposals are to relax an existing standard, benefits are defined as reductions in control costs while costs are defined as increases in environmental damages.

SOURCE: Illinois Institute of Natural Resources. "Economic Impact Studies; Second Year in Review." Docket INR 78-18. February, 1979.

Design Problems in Illinois' Economic Assessment Program

In attempting to fulfill the requirements of the amendments to the Environmental Protection Act, the Institute of Natural Resources has faced a number of problems over the past five years. The nature of these problems and the response to them can shed light on some of the design questions that other states may face when developing an environmental economic assessment program. Some of the more significant design questions raised during Illinois' operating experience are discussed below.

What role should a cost-benefit analysis play in the decision to promulgate a regulation? Debate regarding the proper role of cost-benefit analyses in the state regulatory decision-making process began almost immediately after the amendments creating the program were passed. The two major points of view on the proper use of these studies are described by H. Rowen:[3]

> One [viewpoint] which dominates most of the scholarly literature on the subject, sees it as a method for making choices, a decision rule which enables one to select the most efficient of several alternative courses of action. The other, less often discussed, sees benefit cost analyses as a member of a class of analyses which contributes to the decision processes by assisting in the formulation of objectives and alternative actions, as well as contributing to the process of choice between them.

The first viewpoint implies that cost-benefit study, by presenting cost-benefit ratios or other value indices of alternatives, can in effect determine the optimal regulation. The second viewpoint states that the cost-benefit study is only one factor weighed by the decision maker (in this case, the Illinois Pollution Control Board). Very few witnesses to the Illinois experience would hold the first view of cost-benefit analyses explicitly. The very existence of a hearing process, which essentially allows advocates of alternative positions to give evidence before a regulation is promulgated, is proof that the results of the cost-benefit assessments are not considered as the single, or even primary, determinant in whether to promulgate. Several guideline documents on how to conduct economic impact assessments, prepared by the Institute, have furthermore warned against even presenting cost-benefit ratios or other summary value indices of the proposals brought before the Board.[4]

The straight-forward conclusion regarding the role of cost-benefit analysis, therefore, would be that it was meant to be a part of the decision process. There are, however, difficulties in this point of view. For example, the specification in the Illinois program that an agency separate from the group proposing the regulation develop the economic assessments after the proposal has been submitted to the Pollution Control Board severely limits the role of the economic analysis in the decision process. Since the economic assessment takes place near the end of the decision process, it does not, in a clearly definable way, assist "in the formulation of objectives and alternative action." The independence of the economic analysis from the development of the proposal, however, does allow Illinois industry and environmental groups to be assured that the economic assessment of a specific proposal will be carried out in the most unbiased atmosphere possible. Furthermore, the value of the assessment as evidence in a hearing process is enhanced by a separate agency appraisal.

The difficulty of defining the proper role of economic assessments in Illinois can be stated in terms of a design problem that might affect any state contemplating the initiation of such a program. If the cost-benefit analysis is carried out by those designing the regulations, the economic assessments can be part of the objective formulation and alternative development process and thus can be viewed as an integral part of the decision process, as defined by Rowan. However, in such a situation, the value of an independent analysis is lost. Conversely, if the cost-benefit analysis program is carried out by an agency separate from those designing the regulation, the program does not truly aid in objective development. The tendency of an independent analyst is to view the cost-benefit assessment as a decision rule, that is, as the basis for making decisions. The independent assessor is not participating in a decision process but rather reporting on whether a regulation should or should not be promulgated, based on a comparison of benefits and costs. Even if the analyst wanted to avoid a decision-rule viewpoint, the nature of an independent assessment is to arrive at a conclusion regarding the value of the proposal.

How should long-term economic impacts be assessed? The long-term economic impacts of environmental regulations, such as the influence of regulations on industrial migration, cannot be evaluated easily in a state-level program structured like the Illinois program for a number of reasons. First, long-term economic impacts of environmental regulations will, to a large extent, depend upon the severity of regulations from one state to the next. A state attempting to assess industrial migration would have to predict, not only added pollution control costs to industries within its own boundaries, but also the stringency of future similar regulations in neighboring states. Although federal environmental regulations frequently have tried to neutralize long-run industrial migration incentives by the use of new source performance standards, in environmental regulatory areas in which states have discretion, wide variability in the stringency of regulations from one state to another is possible. Even if an environmental standard is the same for two states, the migrational impact of a regulation on older firms with largely depreciated equipment requiring a significant capital expenditure for pollution controls might be different than for newer plants in other states.

A second difficulty in assessing long-run economic impacts relates to the specific structure of the Illinois program. At present, the Illinois program concentrates its efforts on regulation-by-regulation cost-benefit assessments. This structure of assessment, while serving the needs of the state regulatory body, does not identify the interactive or cumulative effects of the state's entire environmental protection program on a specific industry. It is the combination of environmental pollution costs from all regulations that carries the potential to alter the industrial business climate within a state. Thus, a second general design problem exists. Should a state's economic assessment program seek to service only the needs arising out of the regulatory process, or should the program be more directed towards forecasting longer run impacts resulting from all state environmental protection activities? There is no clear answer to this question.

How many regulatory alternatives should be evaluated in an economic assessment? This question is only relevant if a state has decided that cost-benefit assessments should be conducted by an independent agency. If the economic assessment is conducted by the agency developing the proposal, the number of alternatives considered can be changed as the nature of the proposal changes. When the assessments are done by groups that are not involved in the development of the proposal, such as in the Illinois case, the question of what alternatives need to be evaluated becomes more difficult.

One viewpoint, which has been taken in a number of past Illinois studies, is to consider only two alternatives—either passage of the proposal as it is presented to the Pollution Control Board, or denial of the proposal. If a broader range of regulatory alternatives is to be considered, the question arises as to who should define the proper range of alternatives—the proposing group, the decision maker (the Pollution Control Board), or the Institute of Natural Resources. Since the time and cost of doing the economic assessment will increase as the number of alternatives to be evaluated increases, this question raises yet another design problem for states contemplating initiating a cost-benefit analysis program.

In cases when environmental regulations are essentially federally mandated but require state regulatory action, there is a question whether any alternatives should be evaluated on a state level, or whether a study should be carried out at all. In the particular case of federal preemption, a state agency designing an economic assessment program must ask itself whether one of its functions is to comment on the impact of federal environmental regulations.

How should the benefits of environmental regulations be assessed? The difficulties of environmental benefit assessment are certainly not limited to state programs. The problems of evaluating environmental quality, converting environmental changes to damage impacts, and assigning a monetary value to these impacts have been documented for environmental cost-benefit analyses of regulations at all levels of government. It is not the methodological problems of developing benefit estimates that raise specific issues for a state program; it is rather how such estimates are viewed in the regulatory development process. Initial versions of the Illinois amendments to the Environmental Protection Act did not mention environmental benefits whatsoever. The identification and assessment of pollution control costs were the original objectives of this program. Benefit assessment was, in a sense, an afterthought.

The role of benefit estimation in the Illinois program has been unclear for two reasons. First, benefits related to health impacts are viewed in a significantly different way than those derived from other benefit categories, e.g., recreation, aesthetics, and wildlife preservation. The existence of a variety of health-related pollution concentration standards, most frequently developed under federal auspices, fundamentally alters the way in which health-related impacts are viewed. There is a tendency to ascribe zero dollar damages to situations in which pollution concentrations are below the health standards and infinite dollar damages when such concentrations are above the standards. Basically, a dollar of health benefits is not viewed as equivalent to a dollar of recreational benefit. The strength of what might be termed this "health imperative" will vary, depending upon the regulation under consideration.

A second problem involving the use of benefit estimates concerns their credibility. The required precision of a benefit estimate that reflects the value of the entire federal environmental protection program over a number of years is far different than the precision required to assess the value of a single state environmental regulation. The use of "damage estimates" developed for national studies but applied in a local situation can provide questionable benefit estimates for a state proposal. Furthermore, when national benefit estimates vary by 800 percent, it is not surprising to see a little skepticism on the state level with regard to benefit estimation.

How should state resources be allocated to provide the most effective cost-benefit analysis program? There are a number of areas from a programmatic standpoint that should be considered in developing state guidelines about what regulations should require an environmental cost-benefit analysis and how extensive each analysis should be. The Illinois law requires every proposal brought before the Pollution Control Board to be evaluated. This inflexibility has had the effect of requiring an analysis of regulations that were not controversial, e.g., regulations with administrative impacts only, or limited impacts. Many proposals regarded control measures involving only one plant or community. There has been a tendency for the Illinois program to be involved heavily with the analysis of distributional economic impacts, an area not traditionally part of cost-benefit analysis. This concentration of resources on the assessment of distributional impacts has reduced resources available to develop an overall picture of the economic impacts of the Illinois environmental protection program.

The allocation of effort within a given study is also an area of concern. The Illinois experience has shown that far greater effort has gone into cost estimation activities than into secondary impact or benefit estimation areas. This imbalance may be due to an inherent bias by the engineering contractors performing the analyses to stay in familiar areas. (In estimating pollution control costs, at least the contractor has access to direct information on the market prices of equipment.) Other reasons may include the greater scrutiny that industry generally gives to cost estimates during public hearings or simply a lack of confidence in benefit estimation methods. The effect of this imbalance is to produce economic analyses in which the range of uncertainty in pollution control cost estimates, although sometimes large, is considerably smaller than the uncertainty in benefit or secondary impact estimates. This imbalance of effort reinforces, rather than ameliorates, the uncertainty in benefit estimation.

Thus, the resource allocation question facing states contemplating economic analysis programs can be separated into two facets: which proposals need investigation, and what is the proper division of effort within a given study?

Evaluation of the Illinois Economic Assessment Program

The evaluation of the Illinois economic assessment program must address whether the benefits of the economic impact information developed by the program are worth the costs of the program. Suggestions for structuring such an evaluation were made by T.D. Crocker.[5] Adopting his approach to the assessment of the Illinois program requires answering four questions.

Did the generation of economic impact statements change the type, quality, and quantity of information available to decision makers? Although economic impact analysis had been carried out on occasion before the cost-benefit legislation, the quantity and quality of information available to the Pollution Control Board greatly increased after the assessment program began. This increase was particularly noticeable with respect to secondary economic impacts.

Was this information used in the decision process? In a formal sense, the alteration in the Illinois regulatory procedure to require hearings on economic assessment ensured that such information did enter the decision process.

Did the information alter decisions made by the decision makers? This question is difficult to answer since many factors are considered by the Pollution Control Board. Some evidence does exist, however, that a greater sensitivity to economic factors resulted from the cost-benefit program. An examination of economic issues mentioned in the Board's opinions is indicative of this sensitivity.

As an example, the Pollution Control Board opinion regarding a petition to change water quality, effluent, and sewer discharge standards for cyanide can be cited. The economic impact study concentrated principally on costs and benefits associated with the various effluent standards, generally assuming water quality levels to be a direct function of effluent levels. Several sections of the Board's opinion reveal a sensitivity to the cost-benefit issues raised by the

Institute report. The Board in their opinion wrote: " . . . that the Institute's study presents sufficient data to choose a standard offering adequate environmental protection without requiring unnecessary control and excessive cost."[6]

What is the relationship between the savings resulting from a greater sensitivity to economic impacts and the cost of the economic assessment program? To answer this question, a value must be assigned to the information generated by the program and then be compared with the administrative costs of the program. Based upon budget data from the Illinois Institute of Natural Resources, the administrative costs of the program are approximately $500,000 every year. To compare these costs with potential savings, it is useful to examine the following proposal brought before the Board to relax noise standards for forging plants.[7] Although this proposal reduced control costs by 3 million dollars, it did not significantly change health impacts. This proposal is typical of the type of proposal in which it is fairly easy to identify the dollar value of a program. It is also indicative of the use of cost-benefit analysis to fine tune environmental regulations in an effort to ease the compliance requirements for certain industrial sectors. Only one or two examples (such as the forging noise proposal) more than justify the cost of the program.

In looking at the program from a broader perspective, the pollution control cost to industry resulting from all environmental regulations passed in a year in Illinois has varied from 25 to 100 million dollars. If this level of investment were made in the private sector, a $500,000 assessment of the program's economic reasonableness would be deemed only prudent. Even small improvements in the cost-effectiveness of regulations resulting from cost-benefit studies will easily justify the program.

RECOMMENDATIONS FOR STATE PROGRAMS

The questions that have been raised in this paper only could be formulated after Illinois had developed some experience in its economic analysis program. These questions do not raise methodological problems but rather some issues regarding the structuring, objectives, and use of cost-benefit analysis on a state level. They stress the need for a state, when designing its program, to make compromises about who is to be served by the cost-benefit studies, and how the studies can be employed.

Based upon the history of the Illinois efforts, some general design guidelines can be suggested for states contemplating the initiation of a program parallel to that of Illinois:

- Allow for flexibility in choosing which proposals should be evaluated. If complete discretion by the agency executing the program is not deemed desirable, allow an independent task force or group to select the proposals.

- Determine the value in your situation of having an independent assessment of environmental proposals. If there is not a significant value to this independence (as there is when the analysis is used as evidence in a hearing process), have the economic analysis done at the earliest possible stages of the proposal design by the group developing the proposal.

- Decide the relative priority of serving regulatory agency needs versus establishing the trend of long-term economic impacts of environmental regulations on the state. The structure of the program should follow the establishment of these priorities.

- Determine to some extent, before beginning operation of the program, the role benefit estimation should play. This determination is particularly important for health-related impacts.

- Develop guidelines and a mechanism before an assessment takes place to define the range of alternatives that should be considered.

Notes

1. H. Brickman, "Improving the Analysis of Economic Impacts of State Actions," Office of Development and Planning, Maryland Department of Economic and Community Development, pp. 43-50.

2. Illinois Public Act 80-1218, Section 6.

3. H. Rowan in Henry Peskin and Eugene P. Seskin (eds.), *Cost-Benefit Analysis and Water Pollution Policy* (Washington, D.C.: The Urban Institute, Pub. No. URI 77000, 1973).

4. H. Roberts and H. Sievering, *A Guide to Environmental Benefit Assessments and Economic Impact Studies* (Published by the Illinois Institute of Environmental Quality, Docket No. IIEQ 77-32, 1977).

5. T.D. Crocker in Henry Peskin and Eugene P. Seskin (eds.), *Cost-Benefit Analysis and Water Pollution Policy* (Washington, D.C.: The Urban Institute, Pub. No. URI 77000, 1973).

6. Illinois Pollution Control Board Opinion R74-15, Water Pollution Control Amendment; Cyanide; September 1978, pp. 33-80.

7. Illinois Pollution Control Board Opinion R76-14; Forging Noise.

3/FEDERAL EXPERIENCE

Cost-Benefit Analysis in Federal Environmental Programs

Richard A. Liroff

Those advocating greater use of cost-benefit analysis in federal environmental regulation are adding their voices to the chorus of reformers who for many years have attempted to enhance consideration of costs, benefits, and effectiveness in federal programs. The emphasis of recent reformers has been on the cost of environmental and other social regulations to the private sector. This is somewhat different from reformers' past focus on the costs borne solely by the federal government to implement its many programs. Some of the recent advocacy of cost-benefit analysis is motivated by an urge to improve the cost-effectiveness of federal regulations without unduly compromising the objectives embodied in national environmental laws. But some of it also is prompted by a desire to subvert the nation's commitment to environmental goals.

In February 1981, President Ronald Reagan issued an executive order that: (1) emphasized the importance of measuring the costs and benefits of federal regulations, (2) stressed the significance to be given the resulting analyses, and (3) strengthened the role of the Office of Management and Budget (OMB) to ensure compliance with cost-benefit procedures. To place the president's order in perspective, this essay reviews prior attempts to apply sophisticated analytical techniques to federal programs and examines the impact of past presidential efforts to heighten awareness of the economic effect of regulations. In addition, it reviews the statutory formulae Congress has developed for regulators to consider costs, since some of these statutes will limit the impact of the Reagan order on the Environmental Protection Agency (EPA) and other federal agencies. Finally, it describes EPA's economic assessment activities and suggests some of the difficulties inherent in measuring the costs and benefits of environmental regulations.

PRECEDENTS FOR ECONOMIC ANALYSES

Until the 1970s, cost-benefit analysis in federal programs was applied principally to water resource development projects. The Flood Control Act of 1936, for example, requires benefits to exceed costs for projects such as the dams and navigation systems planned and constructed by the U.S. Army Corps of Engineers. Analyses prepared by the Corps are supposed to be reviewed by the OMB before projects are submitted to Congress for approval.

The Corps' use of cost-benefit analysis has been quite controversial. Environmentalists argue that the Corps has inflated benefits, understated costs, undervalued environmental amenities, and otherwise manipulated quantitative techniques to assure its bureaucratic well-being.[1] Environmentalists have found substantial support for their criticisms from the General Accounting Office, which has issued numerous reports on the mathematical errors, erroneous assumptions, inconsistent methodologies, and other miscalculations made by water resource development agencies.[2] Congress however, has often ignored such critical appraisals of the Corps' calculations. This symbiotic Corps-Congress relationship has produced politically valuable water projects that may be environmentally destructive and that have little economic justification.[3]

In the early 1960s, a major effort to strengthen the analysis of federal programs' costs and benefits was initiated in the Defense Department. The Planning-Programming-Budgeting System (PPBS) established an evaluative process that measured performance in reaching specified policy goals. An effort to extent PPBS throughout the federal government several years later was an utter failure.[4]

PPBS was interred by the early 1970s and replaced by other analytical fads, among them MBO (Management By Objectives) and ZBB (Zero-Based Budgeting).[5] These formal decision systems did not single out particular government programs for analysis but instead were applied across all programs.

PRESIDENTIAL REQUIREMENTS FOR ANALYSIS OF COSTS AND BENEFITS

In the mid-1970s, shortly after environmental statutes proliferated, efforts began to evaluate systematically the economic impacts of major federal regulations. Rising rates of inflation, increasing energy prices, and complaints from those that were regulated all encouraged increased interest in the costs imposed on the private sector by government regulations.

Past Presidential Executive Orders

One of the first programs established to evaluate economic impacts was the inflation impact statement program, created by President Ford in Executive Order No. 11821 issued on November 27, 1974.[6] The purpose of the program was to reduce the inflationary impact of new regulatory and legislative initiatives. Inflation impact statements (later called economic impact statements) were to be prepared for "major" agency proposals, i.e., those expected to have a national economic impact of more than $100 million. The process was to be overseen by the OMB and statements were to be reviewed by staff of the president's Council on Wage and Price Stability (CWPS). Analyses were to include an examination of the cost and inflation effects of proposals, a comparison of estimated costs and benefits, and a review of the costs and benefits of alternatives to the proposals.

The inflation impact statement program was replaced by the Carter administration's regulatory analysis review program. Established by Executive Order 12044, issued on March 23, 1978, the program required agencies to prepare "regulatory analyses" for all regulations either having an annual impact of at least $100 million on the economy or causing a "major" price increase for an industry, level of government, or geographic area.[7] Each analysis had to state the policy problem addressed by the regulation, describe the economic consequences of alternative solutions, and discuss why one particular alternative was preferred. OMB had overall responsibility for the program. Each year, 10 to 20 regulatory analyses were supposed to be selected for review by the Regulatory Analysis Review Group (RARG), which was chaired by the chairman of the Council of Economic Advisors and was staffed largely by personnel from CWPS. Although Executive Order 12044 and the principal OMB memo implementing it did not use the term cost-benefit analysis—referring instead to burdens, gains, and overall economic impact—the practical effect was to encourage use of this technique.[8]

Major industries and others subject to federal regulations supported the Ford and Carter efforts to review costs and benefits, particularly because it is less difficult to measure the costs incurred by industry to comply with regulations than it is to measure the regulations' broadly dispersed benefits to human health.[9] Environmentalists were wary of the reviews by the presidents' economic advisors because reviews sometimes occurred at the last minute or off the record.[10] Most commentators have suggested that the review requirements had little substantive impact. Kathryne Bernick, in a comprehensive examination of President Ford's inflation impact statement program, concluded that it may have improved the use and quality of economic analysis in a few agencies, but it did not curb inflation or affect specific decisions.[11] Bernick attributed the weak impact to inadequate enforcement, to OMB's lack of interest, and the CWPS' limited authority.[12]

The RARG review process depended heavily on President Carter for its success. Unfortunately for RARG, the president's initial enthusiasm did not endure.[13] Following one regulatory squabble, the president signalled that executive reviewers were to function "primarily as kibitzers," rather than as super regulators threatening presidential intercession.[14] One commentator, noting that RARG had examined only 9 of 40 proposals eligible for review, concluded that the program had been long on rhetoric and short on specific results.[15]

In summary, it appears that although the presidential review programs increased cost sensitivity and improved analyses, they did not, except in one or two cases, significantly affect specific regulations.

President Reagan's Regulatory Impact Analysis Program

On February 17, 1981, President Reagan abolished Carter's regulatory analysis program and replaced it with one of his own.[16] Pursuant to Reagan's executive order, OMB has absorbed the roles played by CWPS and RARG and has a much stronger voice in regulatory matters than did its predecessor review agencies. More importantly, the OMB officials involved dislike regulation, as does the president for whom they work.

Reagan's executive order establishes criteria for making and analyzing regulatory decisions, and for clearing regulations and analyses through OMB and through a presidential task force on regulatory relief chaired by the vice president. The Reagan program applies to proposed major rules, i.e., rules meeting the following criteria: (1) rules having an annual effect on the economy of $100 million or more; (2) rules imposing a major increase in costs or prices on particular industries, agencies, consumers, or geographic regions; (3) rules producing significant adverse effects on competition, investment, innovation, and other industrial concerns; and (4) regulations designated as major by the OMB director. The OMB director may also designate existing rules for review.

The executive order states that, to the extent permitted by law, all agencies must adhere to the order's substantive criteria in their regulations. These include: (1) refraining from regulatory action unless potential benefits outweigh potential costs to society; (2) choosing regulatory objectives that maximize net benefits to society; (3) selecting the alternatives that will impose the least net cost to society while achieving regulatory objectives; and (4) setting regulatory priorities to maximize aggregate net benefits to society, taking into account factors such as the condition of the national economy and of particular industries.

The OMB director may prepare and promulgate uniform standards for identifying major rules and developing regulatory impact analyses. Agencies' regulatory analyses must include potential benefits and costs (including nonquantifiable ones), and must identify those likely to bear the benefits and costs. Agencies must include in their analyses alternative policy approaches that would be more cost-effective than their own proposals, with a brief explanation of the legal reasons why such alternatives cannot be adopted. The agencies also must indicate why, if at all, proposed rules cannot be based on the substantive criteria set forth in the preceding paragraph.

The OMB director can review agencies' regulatory documents—proposed rules, preliminary regulatory impact analyses, final rules, and final regulatory impact analyses—prior to the publication of these documents in the Federal Register. The director must provide these reviews within fixed periods specified in the executive order. However, the director also can simply inform the agency within the specified period that he or she intends to submit views on a preliminary rule or impact analysis. The agency, unless otherwise required by statute or court order to publish a proposed rule, must then refrain from publishing until the review is concluded. The agency also must refrain from publishing its final rule and analysis until it has responded to the director's views and incorporated those views and its own response in the rulemaking record.

The executive order also contains miscellaneous provisions that have the effect of postponing the effective date of some pending regulations while exempting others from the provisions of the executive order.

The Reagan executive order, by empowering OMB both to influence rules before their publication and to delay the publication of these rules, resembles the quality of life review established by OMB in 1971. That review, which focused exclusively on EPA, evolved from the concern of some Nixon administration officials about the expanding impact of environmental regulations. The review process required EPA, prior to proposing regulations, to submit these regulations to other agencies for comment. EPA then was required to forward the regulations and comments to OMB, which would review the material and broker differences until issues were resolved. This process had considerable potential to delay or dilute proposals, without the benefit of public review and comment. Following the election of President Carter, EPA unilaterally terminated its compliance with this review process.

Environmentalists and EPA officials initially were concerned about the legality and impact of the quality of life review. Kathryne Bernick, who in 1977 carefully examined the process, found that OMB was able to delay regulations but did not appear to have vetoed any.[17] She concluded that although a process like quality of life review has the potential to be abused by OMB and the White House, during the early 1970s such abuse was narrowly avoided because of the independence of the EPA administrators and the president's lack of interest in environmental affairs.

Some potential exists for abuse of the Reagan program, since the president strongly dislikes regulation, and the new EPA administrator is likely to be less independent than were the EPA administrators in the early 1970s. Because much of the review process will occur without public disclosure, and because it is so difficult to analyze the costs and benefits of specific regulations, some desirable regulations probably will be weakened. While the Reagan program probably will have a greater impact on the substance of EPA regulations than did its predecessors, its ability to delay EPA regulation unduly may be somewhat limited, since 61 percent of the 175 pending EPA regulations are required by statute or court order.[18] The impact of the executive order is examined by Dr. Richard N.L. Andrews in his essay on the politics of cost-benefit analysis.

STATUTORY REQUIREMENTS FOR ANALYSIS
OF COSTS AND BENEFITS

EPA and other executive branch agencies are required by some of their enabling statutes to examine the costs and benefits of regulatory actions. The degree to which these impacts must be examined and weighed varies considerably. Professor William H. Rodgers, Jr., in reviewing the treatment of costs, benefits, and risks in federal environmental and health laws, has placed statutory provisions in four principal categories: cost-oblivious, cost-effective, cost-sensitive, and strict cost-benefit analysis.[19]

The Delaney clause in the Food, Drug and Cosmetic Act, which outlaws additives found to induce cancer in humans or animals, is an example of the cost-oblivious model. A second example is the Clean Air Act's provision for setting national ambient air quality standards, which specifically excludes cost considerations.

Legislators' motives for writing such "cost-oblivious" statutory provisions vary. First, legislators may perform their own intuitive cost-benefit analyses and decide that the benefits of the standards outweigh attainment costs. Second, they may believe that costs outweigh benefits for most but not all types of a particular action, and it is not worth the analytical effort to identify the few exceptions. Third, they may simply make a moral judgment that efficiency considerations are inappropriate and that some minimal level of protection is due the public regardless of the outcome of a cost-benefit analysis. Cost-oblivious provisions in federal statutes are few, and the decisions made under them may occasionally take costs into account implicitly.

In the cost-effective model, Congress establishes a policy goal, and an agency is instructed to select the most efficient means of achieving that goal. Although the most efficient means is often dictated by the marketplace, Congress may prevent an agency from accepting the solution dictated by the marketplace. Congress may perceive the market's seemingly more cost-effective choice as, in fact, less effective and less reliable than a more expensive solution. For example, EPA has been prodded by Congress to require scrubbers on new power plant stacks and has been precluded from accepting the use of more inexpensive but less dependable intermittent controls. In downplaying cost considerations, Congress may believe that emphasizing cost-effectiveness may deter development of innovative technologies, whose initial costs are high and whose benefits are uncertain.

The cost-sensitive model requires that an agency take account of costs, but it does not demand a formal cost-benefit analysis. Statutory provisions in this category may refer to "feasibility" and "practicability." For example, OSHA's occupational health standards must be "feasible," i.e., they cannot bankrupt an industry.

The cost-sensitive and cost-effectiveness models are, according to Rodgers, the dominant congressional ones for considering costs. Rodgers sees these approaches as enabling Congress to postpone hard political choices until, based on initial agency analysis and regulatory action, it has a better understanding of a problem.

"Strict cost-benefit analysis," the fourth model, is required by law for water resource development projects. But even this mandate for cost-benefit analysis is qualified by a requirement that intangible and distributional factors be considered.

These four models define the boundaries within which executive agencies determine how they can comply with OMB's requirements for regulatory analysis. Considerable controversy and some litigation will ensue when agencies assign greater weight to cost concerns than is permitted by statute.

ECONOMIC ANALYSIS WITHIN EPA

EPA produces virtually no formal cost-benefit analyses, *per se*, although it conducts or contracts for many studies of the costs and benefits of its actions. These include:

- macroeconomic analyses employing econometric models, which assess the cumulative impact of pollution control costs on the nation's economy;
- program-specific analyses that assess the impact of a particular pollution control program (e.g., air pollution control) on the nation's economy;
- regulation-specific analyses, performed even when not required by executive order, to give EPA some sense of the economic consequences of its actions;
- industry analyses designed to examine the cumulative impact of multiple environmental regulations on the petroleum, chemical, and other industries;

- issue-specific analyses, performed on an *ad hoc* basis or as required for special reports ordered by Congress;
- plant closings, a quarterly listing of plants closed due to environmental regulations, furnished to the secretary of labor; and
- methods development, designed to improve and test ways of measuring the benefits of pollution control programs.

The foregoing summary of EPA's economic analyses is drawn from a report prepared in 1980 by the Economic Analysis Subcommittee of EPA's Science Advisory Board.[20] The subcommittee contended that cost-benefit analysis has too many uncertainties and too many limitations for it to be relied upon by EPA as the sole basis for decisions. However, the panel also recommended that agencies pay greater attention to costs and benefits. The subcommittee recommended more EPA research on benefits, more prominent display of the trade-offs among regulatory alternatives, and quantification of costs and benefits when possible. The subcommittee recognized that estimates cannot always be monetized but maintained that this should not diminish their weight in decision making. Finally, the subcommittee urged that all estimates of costs and benefits indicate their degree of imprecision and uncertainty.

ANALYTICAL DIFFICULTIES IN ESTIMATING COSTS AND BENEFITS OF POLLUTION CONTROL PROGRAMS

It is extremely difficult to develop sound economic estimates for pollution control programs. A National Academy of Sciences committee, focusing on air pollution control programs, offered a succinct example of some of the problems:

> The basic analysis rests on the determination of the effect of various technologies upon emissions of air pollutants; the effect of changes in emission levels upon ambient air quality; and the effects of changes in air quality on people, vegetation, and materials. An understanding of the state of technology and its reliability and effectiveness, detailed analysis of atmospheric chemistry and transport processes, and consideration of what may be very subtle biochemical relationships that characterize the impact of air pollution on man are necessary. Unfortunately, existing data do not permit clear and unambiguous determination of cause and effect relationships. There are also difficulties in accurately reflecting the costs of new or proposed technologies for pollution control that involve projections based upon uncertain or unavailable information.[21]

The uncertainty of estimates from cost-benefit analysis can sometimes be so large, say its critics, that it cannot contribute as much to rational decision making as some of its proponents may believe. Estimates are especially difficult for controls on carcinogens because of scientific uncertainty over the risks from exposure to these substances. Two particular problems include extrapolating from high to low doses and from nonhuman groups observed in laboratories to the general human population. The saccharin controversy illustrates how great scientific uncertainty can be: one model predicted 5 cancer cases per million persons exposed to saccharin, another predicted 450, another predicted 1200, and a fourth, offered by an industry group, predicted only one death per one billion persons.[22]

The discount rate employed in cost-benefit analyses is another source of considerable uncertainty. The discount rate is used to derive a present dollar value for future costs and benefits. The "appropriate" rate is hotly debated in economic literature and has been a source of controversy in the Corps of Engineers' projects for many years. The rate selected can substantially affect the present value of future costs and benefits, measured in both monetary and non-monetary terms. A report produced by a National Research Council committee on the regulation of chemicals demonstrates how significant the discount rate can be and suggests that the selection of a rate may involve more than mere economic judgments. The committee noted that if a discount rate of 5 percent were used, one case of poisoning by chemicals today would be valued the same as 1,730 cases occurring in 200 years, or over 3 billion cases 450 years hence. The committee concluded that "intergenerational effects of these magnitudes are ethically unacceptable, yet they might be made to appear acceptable if the traditional social rate of discount concept were applied."[23]

Benefit Measurements

In 1980, Dr. A. Myrick Freeman produced for the Council on Environmental Quality (CEQ) a critical review of studies that had estimated benefits from air and water pollution controls in monetary terms. Some of Freeman's findings about the considerable variations in the studies' results were summarized in CEQ's tenth annual report:

> There are a number of reasons for the apparent conflict among the estimates. First, and most fundamentally, different studies have produced dif-

ferent estimates of so-called "dose-response" relationships—that is, the correlation between air pollution and human health or agricultural output; or between water pollution and fish stocks and other aquatic life; or between water quality improvements and swimming, boating, and fishing. Exactly how many illnesses a year, for example, does a given increase in sulfur dioxide and particulate emissions produce? The answers to such questions differ markedly in different studies.

In addition, benefit estimates sometimes differ because physical effects are valued differently. For example, a life saved may be valued according to future lifetime earnings in one study; another study may use an entirely different (and more acceptable) method based on individuals' valuations of risk. Similarly, different studies attribute different values to days off the job on account of illness that may be averted by air pollution control.

Benefit studies differ in simpler ways as well. Some calculate the benefits expected from the eventual full implementation of air and water pollution control laws; others relate benefits only to those environmental improvements already enjoyed; still others are based on some hypothetical improvement in air or water quality. Several studies attempt to make comprehensive, national benefit estimates, while others consider only a single region or concentrate on one particular component of environmental benefits. Some benefits are estimated in 1978 dollars while others use earlier, less inflated dollars as a yardstick.[24]

Freeman standardized the results of the studies by adjusting for a common set of assumptions. But even after expressing estimates in 1978 dollars and standardizing for a 20 percent improvement in air quality, he found that the estimated health benefits of controlling air pollution from stationary sources still ranged from $1.8 billion to $14.4 billion annually.[25] Because the range of estimates was so large, Freeman went further and selected a "most reasonable point estimate" for air and water pollution control benefits. He then concluded: "Where state of the art analyses of environmental benefits have been undertaken ... they strongly suggest that environmental protection is good economics."[26]

The ratio of benefits to costs for some pollution control programs is hotly contested. In late 1980, National Economic Research Associates (NERA) completed a report for the Business Roundtable on the costs and benefits of air pollution control. After examining evidence to support statements by EPA and CEQ that expenses of $400 billion by 1985 would be more than justified by the benefits achieved, NERA countered with its estimate that "the probable benefits are about one half the costs."[27]

Cost Measurements

It is often assumed that it is harder to estimate the benefits of controlling pollution than to estimate the costs, but the difficulty of accurately estimating costs is indicated by a recent EPA study that reviewed actual and estimated compliance costs for several industries and standards.[28] The report concluded that both EPA and industry tended to overestimate the cost of compliance, although EPA's estimates tended to be lower than industries' estimates.

The EPA study reviewed six cases: the cost of compliance with effluent guidelines for the pulp and paper industry, the petroleum refining industry, the iron and steel industry, and electric utilities; the cost of scrubbers to electric utilities; and the cost of automotive emission controls.

EPA overestimated the cost of complying with effluent guidelines for the paper, refining, and steel industries and underestimated the costs for utilities. Industry, on the other hand, underestimated costs for the paper industry and overestimated costs for the other three industries. Both EPA and industry underestimated the cost of scrubbers.

EPA was more accurate than industry in estimating the impact of catalytic converters and other auto emission controls on sticker prices. Auto industry estimates ranged from a 50 percent underestimate to a 130 percent overestimate. One explanation of the overestimates was the early expectation that large amounts of expensive platinum would be required for catalytic converters. Because of design improvements, actual costs were lower than estimated costs. This experience lends support to the view that there is danger in projecting costs in a situation in which technology is dynamic.

Variations in these forecasts stemmed from a combination of different assumptions regarding unit control costs, the amount of capacity affected, industrial growth rate, and rate of program implementation. The EPA study containing these findings has itself been questioned because it excludes operating costs and because the consultants who prepared it have adjusted the data. The study's findings suggest how difficult it can be to assess accurately the costs of proposed regulations.

CONCLUDING OBSERVATIONS

EPA has conducted many assessments of costs and benefits, on its own initiative, in response to congressional requirements, and in accordance with executive orders. The EPA analyses sometimes disagree sharply with those produced by other interested parties. Some of the disagreements may result from varying personal and institutional values; others may simply reflect the enormous uncertainty inherent in measuring the impact of complex programs over long time periods.

EPA does not use formal cost-benefit analysis in its economic impact assessments, nor should it. But a careful examination of costs and benefits, with adequate resources devoted to measuring benefits, may advance environmental quality goals. Since the nation's resources for reducing health risks and preventing environmental harms are finite, sensitivity to both costs and benefits may help us to realize the greatest environmental and health gains from our expenditures. However, this does not mean that a ceiling should be placed on environmental and health spending.

Those who are so vociferous in calling for an analysis of the costs and benefits of environmental regulations should be equally insistent in calling for close economic scrutiny of federal programs that may be environmentally harmful. An example of one such program is the synthetic fuels program that the federal government has chosen to fund. Many energy specialists contend that far greater energy benefits, at far less economic and environmental cost, could be derived by directing this federal investment toward energy conservation. Similarly, the enormous federal subsidy (e.g., insurance, disaster aid, and public works) for development on barrier islands and other flood-prone areas should perhaps be eliminated, because these federal expenditures encourage unwise development in environmentally sensitive areas.

Public support for environmental protection remains strong despite inflationary pressures, energy problems, and efforts to scapegoat environmental regulations for economic problems.[29] However, this support is potentially subject to erosion, Three Mile Island and Love Canal notwithstanding, if no systematic effort is made to promote cost-effectiveness in environmental regulation. Monetized cost-benefit analysis should not be the rule by which EPA's decisions are made, but some regime for promoting rigorous analysis of benefits and costs and examining alternative regulations might help shore up the public's confidence in environmental programs and the public's willingness to bear their costs.

Analysis of the costs and benefits of environmental regulation may improve resource allocations and build public support, but if information from those with an economic stake in regulation is perceived as dominating the evaluation processes, government decisions may lose some of their legitimacy. Developing more flexible, cost-sensitive regulations is one way of getting government "off the back" of those it regulates, but reform of the regulatory process must not land government in the pocket of the regulated.

Notes

1. See Chapter 6 in Walter A. Rosenbaum, *The Politics of Environmental Concern* (New York: Praeger Publishers, 2d ed., 1977).

2. In a 1978 report, GAO commented that "we believe. . . a major contributing factor in cost-benefit practices has been the influences from Federal, State, and local levels as well as the self-interest of the agencies preparing the analysis. A real change is needed in the system to insure the development of more objective and impartial benefit-cost ratios." See Comptroller-General of the United States, "An Overview of Benefit-Cost Analysis for Water Resources Projects—Improvement Still Needed" (Washington, D.C.: U.S. General Accounting Office Report No. CED-78-127, August 7, 1978), page 28.

3. Rosenbaum, *supra* note 1.

4. See Aaron Wildavsky, *The Politics of the Budgetary Process* (Boston: Little, Brown and Co., 2d. ed., 1974).

5. For some reviews of initial federal efforts to implement zero-base budgeting, see "Zero-Base Budgeting: It Made a Difference," *New York Times,* January 22, 1978, and "Zero Base Budgeting Gets Mixed Reviews," *Washington Post,* November 13, 1977. A later *Washington Post* report on the first year's experience said the program had "increased paperwork substantially without producing any dramatic cutback in spending." See "White House Rates ZBB: Good But Can Be Better," *Washington Post,* May 3, 1973. The initial OMB guidelines for the process were published at 42 Fed Reg. 22342 (May 2, 1977).

6. 39 Fed. Reg. 41501 (1974), as amended by Executive Order 11949, 42 Fed. Reg. 1017 (1977).

7. 43 Fed. Reg. 12661 (March 23, 1978).

8. The characterization of the Executive Order's practical effect is Michael Baram's. See "Cost-Benefit Analysis: An Inadequate Basis for Health, Safety and Environmental Regulatory Decisionmaking," 8 *Ecology L.Q.* 473, 509 (1980).

9. See Christopher DeMuth, "The White House Review Programs," *Regulation* (January/February 1980), page 27.

10. See the comments of Natural Resource Defense Council's Richard Ayres, in U.S. Congress, Senate Committee on Environment and Public Works, Subcommittee on Environmental Pollution, "Executive Branch Review of Environmental Regulations," 96th Congress, 1st Sess., 1979, Serial No. 96-H4, page 27.

11. Kathryne Bernick, "The Inflation Impact Statement Program and Executive Branch Coordination," (Draft Report prepared for American Bar Association Commission on Law and the Economy, May 1977). The author's permission to cite this work is gratefully acknowledged.

12. *Id.* But Baram contended that CWPS had demonstrated a disturbing ability to influence safety standards and delay agency action by using economic studies laden with arbitrary assumptions that transcended economic expertise. See Baram, *supra* note 8, page 507.

13. The importance of presidential support was cited by Susan Tolchin. See "Presidential Power and the Politics of RARG," *Regulation* (July/August 1979), page 45.

14. DeMuth, *supra* note 9, page 20.

15. Id. This conclusion also was reached by journalist Timothy Clark. See "The Costs and Benefits of Regulation—Who Knows How Great They Really Are?" *National Journal* (December 1, 1979), page 2027.

16. Executive Order 12291, 46 Fed. Reg. 13193 (1981).

17. Kathryne Bernick, "Executive Branch Coordination: The Quality of Life Review," (Draft Report prepared for American Bar Association Commission on Law and the Economy, September 1977). The author's permission to cite this work is gratefully acknowledged.

18. The EPA analysis is reported in Timothy B. Clark, "OMB to Keep its Regulatory Powers in Reserve in Case Agencies Lag," *National Journal* (March 14, 1981), page 428.

19. William H. Rodgers, Jr., "Benefits, Costs and Risks: Oversight of Health and Environmental Decisionmaking," 4 *Harvard Environmental L. Rev.* 191 (1980).

20. U.S. Environmental Protection Agency, Science Advisory Board, Subcommittee on Economic Analysis, "Economics in EPA" (Washington, D.C., June 1980). This report offers some specific examples of the studies mentioned in the text.

21. National Academy of Sciences, Committee on Environmental Decision-Making, "Decision-making in the Environmental Protection Agency—Volume II" (Washington, D.C., 1977), page 27.

22. This example is cited in James P. Leape, "Quantitative Risk Assessment in Regulation of Environmental Carcinogens," 4 *Harvard Environmental L. Rev.* 86, 103 (1980).

23. National Academy of Sciences, "Decision Making for Regulating Chemicals in the Environment," (Washington, D.C., 1975), page 43.

24. U.S. Council on Environmental Quality, "Environmental Quality—1979" (Washington, D.C.: Government Printing Office, 1979), page 654.

25. *Id.*

26. A. Myrick Freeman, "The Benefits of Air and Water Pollution Control: A Review and Synthesis of Recent Estimates" (Report prepared for the U.S. Council on Environmental Quality, December 1979), page XII.

27. See Air/Water Pollution Report, December 1, 1980, page 475.

28. See Putnam, Hayes, and Bartlett, Inc., "Comparison of Estimated and Actual Pollution Control Costs for Selected Industries" (Report prepared for U.S. EPA Office of Planning and Evaluation, February 1980).

29. See U.S. Council on Environmental Quality, "Public Opinion on Environmental Issues—Results of a National Public Opinion Survey" (Washington, D.C.: Government Printing Office, 1980).

Part III
SOURCES OF THE CONTROVERSY

4/INTRODUCTION

Cost-Benefit Analysis in Environmental Regulation: Sources of the Controversy

Daniel Swartzman

The following dialogue between Messrs. Price and Worth presents some of the often-heard arguments for and against the use of cost-benefit analysis in environmental regulation. It also illustrates the different levels of such a discussion and the often-seen inability of participants to communicate effectively.[1]

Worth: "The use of cost-benefit analysis to value human life is morally and intellectually irresponsible."

Price: "But what would you have us do otherwise? Ordinary political standard-setting, which dictates the types of products that must be sold or the processes that must be used, interferes with consumer choice and impedes producer flexibility. To the extent these requirements deviate from what rational planning and analysis would recommend, as they inevitably do, these restrictions on choice and conduct are clearly undesirable."

Worth: "The very act of 'rational analysis,' when it focuses on monetized values, can distort significantly and detrimentally the decision-making process you are trying to improve."

Price: "I'm not suggesting that cost-benefit analysis be a decision rule. It's a useful tool that allows us to organize and express certain kinds of information on the range of alternative courses of action. It also indicates how far our intended regulations deviate from a market-generated optimum."

Worth: "Human life is priceless. One characteristic of priceless goods is that they can't be bought and sold. If, in fact, they are being marketed, then it follows that the market has overstepped its legitimate bounds."

Price: "Whether you believe the results or not, a cost-benefit analysis improves decision making. You always know more about a project when you've done an analysis."

Worth: "But the very use of the market for steering production and allocation of a 'thing' imposes a cost. Similarly, when you use cost-benefit analysis to measure something, you adversely affect the value you are trying to measure. Besides, the public won't stand for the improved decision process you suggest. It's like the park superintendent who has done a cost-benefit study on how many children must die on diving boards before it is optimal for the park district to act. Such a man has so distanced himself from human feelings that he could not be trusted not to do something outrageous."

Price: "I'll concede that some past work valuing human lives has been shown to be nonsense. Unfortunately, as a result, too many decision makers now shy away from any attempt to value, in terms of dollars, the benefits of environmental and other costly programs."

Worth: "The present drive for deregulation shows we lack confidence in the ability of appointed and independent 'experts' to reach the correct balance between social goals and economic costs. Given the level of uncertainty in cost-benefit analyses, judgment of the analyst becomes critical. But these decisions that reduce uncertainty are transscientific, involving important values that should not be left solely to the personal judgments of experts."

Price: "Surely you aren't suggesting that Congress directly regulate these issues. There's a serious danger that its decisions would become more heavily politicized than they are now in the hands of administrative agencies. But I agree with you that we need to create a system for continuous political monitoring of all government regulation to ensure its responsiveness to the changing economic and social needs of the country. However, that political function can be dealt with separately from objective economic analysis."

Worth: "Politics and analysis are not so easily separated. Most important analyses raise issues of political participation. For example, should economic analyses done after promulgation of a regulation be subject to public notice and comment? Furthermore, every move toward political responsiveness raises more analytical issues. Should the economic impacts of a one-house veto be subject to a cost-benefit analysis?

But we've departed from the central issue—intrinsic value. Your economic analyses have forced environmentalists to phrase their arguments in terms of human self-interest as measured in dollars. By articulating environmental goals wholly in these terms, you are asking the environmentalist to legitimize a system of discourse that so structures human thought and feeling as to erode, over the long run, the very sense of obligation to nature that provided the initial impetus for his or her own protective efforts."

Price: "Look, all I am arguing for is effective and optimal resource utilization. An objective cost-benefit analysis will only help."

Worth: "You assume that effective utilization would mirror the results of human self-interest. Regulation as a substitute for the invisible hand. What about altruism as a model, rather than economic incentives? It would be incredibly difficult and costly to set up a system in which economic incentives would make it in people's self-interest to behave appropriately when self-interest would not do so otherwise. Social interaction would come to a standstill. As for optimality, isn't it more important to resolve controversy than to produce an objectively correct result? I know this offends the engineer in you, but it's possible that 'optimum' resolution of a controversy may require us to accept as true something that we know is untrue. And as for usefulness, detailed descriptions of analytical techniques are less useful and less relevant to the public policy decision maker than a clear, concise explanation of the unknowns, the possible sources of error, and estimated magnitudes."

Price: "Without technical analysis, your decision maker is just
         making a subjective estimate. The public should be edu-
         cated as to the fallibility of such subjective estimates of
         risk. We have to replace these with some objective mea-
         sures of risk."

Worth: "For all your claims of value neutrality, let's face it, the so-
         called objectivity of the policy sciences is a myth. You
         can't escape subjective values in policy decision making.
         Analysis can never substitute for wisdom, good judg-
         ment, and compassion."

Price: "But cost-benefit analysis isn't intended to replace subjec-
         tive decisions. It is an attempt to make explicit the balanc-
         ing judgments we all make every day."

Worth: "Do we really? Your analysis establishes numerical in-
         dices for the actual underlying social values many of us
         hold. We can't lose sight, however, of the difference be-
         tween the underlying reality and the explicit index. The
         clarity and apparent objectivity of quantitatively measur-
         able subordinate goals can easily lead to our failure to
         bear in mind that these goals are in fact subordinate."

Price: "We've reached a point where we need to consider basic
         philosophical orientations, such as whether we want a
         technologically conservative society, which proceeds into
         areas of risk only with empirical demonstration of safety,
         or a gambling, venturesome society, which leaps boldly
         into new areas in full confidence of its ability to meet un-
         expected challenges."

Worth: "Certainly cost-benefit analysis won't help us do much
         leaping. If your tools of monetization, forecasting, and
         discounting of future benefits had been in vogue 80 years
         ago, the Wright brothers would have been convinced not
         to pursue their dream. How can you get around the unre-
         alistic economic assumptions, the measurement difficul-
         ties, the subjectivity of choosing a discount rate, and the
         questionable political and philosophical positions that
         cost-benefit analysis entails? Cost-benefit analyses make
         judicial review of agency decisions difficult and public as-
         sessment impossible. These analyses are reductionistic,
         while environmental problems are inherently holistic.

They are irretrievably anthropocentric; they incorporate the view that man holds dominion over nature. Most significantly, while we are faced with normative decisions of what ought to be, you offer an approach whose practitioners take pride in their inability to say what we should do."

Price: "While I think you are being a touch histrionic in your attack, for the moment, let's grant the truth of what you say. Do you propose we solve the difficult, critical, monumental resource allocation questions facing us by blind intuition exercised by ignorant, over-worked, and politically motivated legislators? I ask you, if not cost-benefit analysis, then what?

THE CONTROVERSY

To those readers involved in developing environmental public policy, as advocates, decision makers, or analysts, the foregoing discussion is probably familiar. The controversy over the use of cost-benefit analysis in establishing environmental regulation is fully engaged.[2] It is a controversy that sometimes inspires high emotions and low blows. Dialogues often involve as little communication, and end as fruitlessly, as the one just presented.

This paper examines that controversy and offers a model for understanding the principal sources of disagreement.[3] From that understanding may flow a resolution of these disputes or at least the improved communication to enable discussants to reach some areas of agreement while focusing remaining areas for further discussion.

Previous attempts to categorize the principal sources of disagreement have not been completely successful. Ashford, et al., differentiate among the "philosophical, conceptual, analytical and practical issues that limit the potential utility of benefit analysis."[4] Richard Merrill divides the sources of controversy into (1) institutional and political constraints and (2) methodological constraints.[5] Others separate the methodological issues from the ethical issues.[6]

Despite these efforts, distinctions among categories remain muddled. For example, some writers who view attempts to put a monetary value on human life as inappropriate state this ethical view in the midst of a discussion of the actual difficulties of such quantification.[7] Michael Baram calls the question of setting the discount rate

for environmental decisions an "ethical problem that transcends economic and legal perspectives."[8] Ben-David, et al., say that setting
the rate is a matter of temporal distribution,[9] of who gets what share
of the benefits. Authors frequently mix a discussion of poorly done
analyses with arguments about what analysis should not do.[10] One
writer has labeled some controversial issues as "practical" problems.[11] Another writer seems not to care whether his arguments can
be categorized at all.[12]

It is the thesis of this discussion that an improved categorization
of the sources of controversy is possible and will facilitate communication among these concerned with the costs and benefits of U.S.
environmental policy. The following discussion briefly introduces
the proposed taxonomy. It then examines more closely the components of the taxonomy and provides, for each source of controversy, examples based on Illinois' five years of experience in writing
and evaluating "economic impact statements" on all proposed environmental regulations.

SOURCES OF THE CONTROVERSY

The three sources of controversy offered here are: methodology,
politics, and ethics. Methodological issues concern how cost-
benefit analyses can be done. Political issues center on how we are
to use the analyses in making decisions. The major ethical question
is: "Should we conduct these analyses at all?"

That rhetorical hammer to which so many writers on public policy have referred may help illustrate the differences among, and
demonstrate the discreteness of, the three categories. If given a
hammer, you might begin using it by holding onto the head and
pounding the nail with the handle. Or you might hold it correctly
but endeavor to drive the nail with a lateral blow. If someone were
to argue with you about how the nail actually should be driven,
that individual would be introducing a discussion of methodology.

If, on the other hand, you pound on other people's nails without
asking, it is not the method that might be questioned, but the use to
which you were putting the tool. Concerns that involve who pays
for the nails and who benefits from the hammering, whether the
hammering is generally accepted as worth doing, what the real motivation for the hammering is, e.g., whether you actually intend to
drive nails or are using that as an excuse to make a lot of noise, are
termed political issues.

If, however, someone were to tell you that you ought not to be using the hammer at all, no matter how well you wield it, or to what use you put it, or that your hand will get dirty by using the tool, that would be an ethical argument.

It should be clear that the proposed use of these descriptive terms does not fit perfectly with their current usage in cost-benefit analysis literature. Many writers would say that the setting of a discount rate is as much an ethical question as is valuing a human life.[13] However, the discount rate issue is actually a matter of distributing costs and benefits over time. The equitable distribution of benefits is a fundamental concern of our political system. The issue is not whether it is wrong to set a discount rate, but whether we want to use cost-benefit analysis to make these distributional judgments. Commentators have discussed the methodological problems of assigning a dollar value to human longevity, but arguments against doing so have their foundations in whether this should be done at all, regardless of methodological sophistication.

It is important to understand these distinctions, since the inability to move toward resolution of the controversy is likely a function of each discussant viewing the problem from a different perspective. An economist will support work to further the state-of-the-art while an environmental health advocate decries the pricing of human worth. The business leader will ask for government analyses that examine the efficiency of regulation, while the politically accountable legislator wishes to preserve his or her constituents' rightful share of the pie. These methodology/ethics and methodology/politics clashes can be difficult to resolve. Differences in perspective frustrate communication. Resolution is impossible when the differences result in participants speaking in foreign tongues, trying to trade currencies for which no exchange rate exists.

METHODOLOGY

Methodological disputes are many and varied. Ideally, the decision maker would like a tool to predict changes in the quality of life or in the standard of living.[14] Methodological questions examine how well cost-benefit analysis can make these predictions.[15] The following, typical of issues that arise from this source of controversy, is not intended to be an exhaustive list but rather to illustrate the types of issues that arise in methodological disputes.

- Measurement: Since analysts often are asked to measure things that have no ready-made index (value of visibility, for example), they must look for indicators. The adequacy of these indicators and the techniques used (surveys or "revealed perference" studies) are controversial. Is the correct measure of loss to an individual the amount necessary to compensate him or her, or the amount he or she would be willing to pay to avoid the loss?[16]

- Uncertainty: Problems of uncertainty can arise from sampling techniques or from ignorance about biological mechanisms.[17] Accounting procedures, financial forecasting techniques, technological innovation, and diffusion and learning curves all give rise to uncertainty.[18] Sometimes uncertainty can be so great as to make a quantified analysis useless.[19]

- Data: A quantified analysis is no better (although sometimes worse) than the quality and quantity of data available. Most analyses are extremely data-limited, often because of the high cost of generating information. Usually much of the information comes from the industry or other private concern that is the subject of regulation.[20] Most analyses must rely on aggregated data, which can obscure important population profile questions.[21] At the extreme, some data needed for valid and reliable cost-benefit work "are not just unknown, but unknowable . . . ."[22]

- Linkages: Important information involving linkages among the various elements of environmental damage often is missing. For instance, in making decisions on the impact of reduced emissions of industrial pollutants on human health costs, the analyst does not have available all of the data linking fuel input to emission rates to ambient concentrations to exposure rates to dosage to response rate to health impact to costs.

- Judgment: Judgments and assumptions made by the analyst are inevitable, particularly in light of the problems mentioned above.[23] Controversy arises most often when the analyst fails to make these decisions explicit[24] or fails to discuss the significance of the judgments.[25] Critics have challenged the professionalism and the ethical conduct of some analysts,[26] suggesting that judgments allow the preparer of a cost-benefit analysis to prejudice the results.[27] (An argument could be made that the source of this controversy is the "politics" dimension,[28] but the problem is close enough to the question of making judgments and assumptions explicit that it merits mentioning here.)

- Fractionalization: Some analyses tend to fractionalize the benefits of a proposed regulation. This may result from a number of agencies each comparing total costs of compliance to the small portion of benefits that falls within its jurisdiction,[29] or from comparing costs of compliance and the correspondingly small net decrease in pollution from only one source, without evaluating costs of the aggregate pollution problem from all sources of that type.[30]

The Illinois Experience

These issues are typical of those that have confronted the Illinois Pollution Control Board in its effort to use cost-benefit analysis in environmental regulation. Since 1975, every regulatory proceeding before the Illinois Pollution Control Board has involved preparation, presentation, cross-examination, and formal consideration of an "economic impact statement."[31] Those involved in the preparation and review of these documents have observed many of the methodological problems cited above. Contractors admit that their analyses are often not state-of-the-art or are of limited sophistication because the cost of doing such a single statement thoroughly would likely take an inordinate share of the budget allocated to the entire economic impact statement program in Illinois.[32]

Analysts usually rely on data presented by the regulated private concern. They take pains to make this clear in their reports, but the limitations are obvious. For example, in one proceeding on relaxing carbon monoxide emission limitations for steel plants, all of the technical work, modeling, and economic analyses were based on pollution data supplied by the steel companies. The economic impact statement attempted to advance the state-of-the-art in estimating dollar benefits from carbon monoxide controls,[33] but the sophisticated analysis was given little attention because the proponents and opponents spent most of their time arguing over the validity of the data.

Many of the analyses prepared for proceedings involving water pollution from a single source fall prey to the fractionalization problem. Typically, the analyst computes the costs of compliance for a particular plant and then avers that the relatively small water pollution loading from the plant would not significantly increase health or welfare costs in the state.[34] Plant by plant, this could be true. But analysts have yet to reverse the process—to attempt the more meaningful analysis of computing total water quality costs in Illinois and then estimate the relevant fraction that would be attributable to the plant at hand.

The linkages problem also has occurred regularly. In an analysis of proposed controls on the emissions of volatile organic compounds from stationary sources, the preparer of the report chose not to estimate the health benefits of the proposal, primarily because of the inability to make the necessary linkages in forecasting air quality and public health impacts.[35] In addition to this problem, levels of uncertainty have been so great in water quality reports that the preparers also have chosen not to estimate levels of benefits, much less a dollar value.[36]

Two problems, which the literature has not addressed, that have arisen in Illinois' experience are standardization and contractor comprehensiveness. The Illinois Institute of Natural Resources (IINR), which administers the economic impact program, had hoped to make the documents more useful to the Pollution Control Board (the decision makers) by providing some standardization in format and presentation.[37] However, the Board was concerned that this might stifle innovation,[38] and the effort for standardization has been dropped.

Most of the economic impact statements prepared under the enabling legislation that set up this program are contracted out by the IINR to private consultants or to academic institutions. This has created the problem of finding a contractor adept at analyzing such diverse fields as pollution engineering, meteorology, environmental medicine, and economics.[39] While this, like all the problems mentioned above, is becoming rarer as the program matures, similar methodological problems can be expected whenever such projects are undertaken.

To illustrate the impact of methodological problems and decisions, consider the economic impact analyses of a proposed rule to limit noise pollution from motor vehicle racing within Illinois.[40] The private consultant hired to do the analysis found that the total costs of the proposal would be $797,770. The report included a benefits estimate of $424,877.[41] The Illinois Environmental Protection Agency (IEPA), proponents of the regulation, disputed these figures. Conducting their own analysis, IEPA estimated costs at only $183,200 and benefits at $1,602,000. The disparity, due to different methods, different assumptions, and different data, was significant. The contractor computed a cost-to-benefit ratio of 2:1, while the agency arrived at a cost-to-benefit ratio of 1:9.[42]

The IINR is making a concerted effort to overcome these difficulties. However, many questions remain:

- Will the state legislature ever be willing to commit the funds necessary to overcome the financial limits of these analyses? Will it ever be possible to collect data independent of the regulated industry?

- Will analysts be able to develop risk assessment and sensitivity analysis techniques sophisticated enough to make useful projections in the face of missing linkages and high levels of uncertainty?

- Will the judgments and assumptions made by contractors be handled through the Board's hearing process (as is done today) or can analysts develop methods for incorporating these judgments and assumptions more vividly into their reports?

POLITICS

Commentators have argued repeatedly that cost-benefit analysis should not be the basis of environmental decision making.[44] They maintain that "regulation today involves political choices between competing interests—concerning which economic and social goals to pursue, how far and at what economic and social costs."[45] The market-type "voting" behavior captured by economic analysis is fundamentally different from the political voting behavior that is the ultimate basis of public decision making. The former is more "individualistic" and the latter more "communalistic."[46] Making political decisions using only economic tools fails to reflect these important differences.

What separates a technical, economic analysis from the political judgment-making process of an administrative agency or a legislature? Why is an agency not able to make a purely technical, analytic policy decision? Behind that question is "the notion that there is a discoverable, unitary and nonpolitical truth called 'the public interest.'"[47] The trouble is "that political concerns interfere with the objective search for this truth."[48]

There is a fundamental split in the world view embodied by what Robert Reich has called the "economic impact critique" and the "political responsiveness critique" of agency decisions.[49] The former tries to cast agency decisions into objective fact-finding exercises, while the latter sees the goal of the decision as a function of the specific regulatory proceeding (a function of the issues, the actors, the setting). Reich has identified a basic faultline that cleaves politics from economics, equity from efficiency, conflict resolution from resource optimization, consensus from objective solutions, and lawyers from engineers.

The world view of the analyst is founded in positivism, that philosophical position which presumes an objective and absolute truth transcending human experience.[50] The politician is a relativist; truth is a function of circumstances, a matter of context.[51] A full exploration of the impact of these divergent views is well beyond the scope of this essay, but a recognition of this basic split will aid in understanding how controversies arise from "politics." The three issues of controversy discussed in this essay are: (1) distributing resources equitably, (2) preserving democratic decision making, and (3) preventing misuse of the analyses.

Distribution of Resources

Professor Stephen Breyer, in his analysis of governmental regulation, takes to task government intervention that attempts to meet political goals beyond what the action was designed to accomplish.[52] However, as George Schultz points out,[53] government and business have different ways of doing things. Business looks for efficiency, while government strives for the equitable means to its ends. "Society uses decision rules other than economic efficiency to judge the worth of regulatory programs; equity and fairness are also important."[54]

Equity or equitable distribution is the decision rule most often juxtaposed with efficiency. Although efficiency generates savings, if the savings are not used to benefit those who stand to lose for efficiency's sake, then society may often opt for a less cost-effective, but more equitable, option.[55] Governmental equity considerations seek to determine who gets the pieces of the pie and how big each person's share is. Cost-benefit analysis as currently practiced has little to say on this question.[56]

An example of the distribution issue as it currently is dealt with in cost-benefit analysis is the discount rate. It has become *de rigueur* to speak of discount rates in any critique of cost-benefit analyses, but the question of whether to apply a discount rate to future-incurred costs or benefits (and, if so, which rate) usually is dealt with as a methodological or an ethical issue.[57] Under the model presented in this paper, however, the discount rate controversy can actually be viewed as a political question of equitable distribution over time. Unless the policy maker intends to set aside money as an investment to apply as amelioration for losses incurred in the future, then discounting acts to distribute benefits today, paid for tomorrow.[58] The decision involves the classic political issue of pie slicing and pie distributing.

It will be necessary in further discussions to address how to use cost-benefit analyses within the context of political distribution and equity problems because "ultimately the effectiveness, efficiency, and fairness of individual policy decisions depend on political factors."[59]

Democratic Decision Making

Environmental policy decisions are political decisions[60] and are, therefore, "most appropriately made by officials who are politically accountable and through procedures that permit public participation."[61] According to Professor Harold Green, the governmental decision maker "does not know, and cannot reliably ascertain, what mix of benefits is desired by the public. He decides on the basis of experience, intuition, and perception, and is politically accountable for the quality of his decisions."[62]

The processes this country chooses to use in making environmental decisions are not always compatible with the rigid analytic process employed by policy planners. For instance, agency regulatory hearings and judicial review both are adversarial processes that seek to resolve conflict rather than achieve objective truth.[63] Policy analysts are positivists. Policy makers are usually relativists. The underlying cause of this tension may be inevitable conflicts of human nature.[64] Whatever the cause, the problem of folding a cost-benefit analysis into a democratic decision-making process is a thorny one and raises many questions.

Some fear that policy makers may abrogate their political responsibility in favor of the "supposedly objective formalism"[65] of cost-benefit analysis. "This provision of an escape hatch from accountability is a particularly pernicious distortion of the democratic process."[66] Others have attempted to reconcile the two impulses into a systematic determination of "risk acceptability."[67] However, these attempts at infusing policy making with objectivity seldom fully escape the need for subjective judgment.[68]

Information overload, to which cost-benefit analyses can contribute, forces the decision maker to limit the agenda for inquiry. This can have profound and unfortunate effects.[69] Possible solutions of an environmental problem may be limited to those that can be translated easily into mathematical equations, rather than creative and promising options that are not readily analyzable in the appropriately quantified manner.

Baram argues convincingly that a careless use of analyses may substantially harm the accessibility, responsiveness, and accountability of EPA decision making.[70] Breyer points out that the rules of combat set forth by regulators to ensure democratic values often make it difficult for regulators to have enough flexibility to develop economically efficient standards.[71] Amory Lovins suggests that, in addition to the accountability problem, cost-benefit analyses will enhance the elitist nature of government decisions, undermine the open nature of those decisions, and replace simple, political judgments with "pseudo-scientific snow."[72]

Deciding how to use cost-benefit analyses in environmental decisions will force legislatures, agencies, and courts to review the decision rules they have adopted. For instance, Congress must decide the level of consideration to be given to costs and benefits. William Rodgers has said that the four levels Congress has established to date range from "cost-oblivious" through "cost-effective" and "cost-sensitive" to true "cost-benefit."[73] He also points to three standards of judicial review that the courts may apply or already have applied.[74] He and David Doniger both discuss changes in allocating the burden of persuasion as a mechanism for accommodating cost-benefit issues within the adversary process.[75]

Even if all of the methodological questions were to be answered, the foregoing discussion shows the difficulty of using cost-benefit analyses within the context of democratic decision-making processes. Such use opens a gap between economic theory and the reality of public decision making. And from the gap between theory and practice arises the problems of integrating cost-benefit analysis into environmental policy making.[76]

Misuse

A third controversial issue resulting from how the hammer is used is the problem of misuse or abuse. Even if the analyses are done perfectly, and even if they are melded in to equitable, democratic decision making, there is still the possibility of negligent or willful misuse. The reasons for this are many. The financial rewards to participants in a regulatory proceeding for successfully tailoring pollution standards to their needs can be very high.[77] Cost-benefit analysis involves a variety of techniques that many of the participants do not understand, or worse, understand only partially. Ruth Ruttenberg of the Occupational Safety and Health Administration (OSHA) uses an amazing eight-pointed, multi-rhomboid model to demonstrate how few of the many important facets of a regulatory strategy are actually dealt with by most cost-benefit analysis.[78]

This discussion cannot identify all of the myriad ways ingenious minds can conjure to misuse or abuse cost-benefit analysis. A few examples may suffice to indicate why controversies arise from this problem.

Lovins argues that these analyses are often creatures of decisions already made rather than tools with which to forge the decision.[79] Hence, analysts, either wittingly or unwittingly, subtly bias the analysis by assuming decision parameters that restrict the results of the process. Myrick Freeman cautions the readers of his recent book[80] that the cost-benefit numbers take on a life of their own in public discourse "where qualifications and limitations tend to be ignored."[81] Mendeloff demonstrates how agency decisions are subject to powerful forces and counterforces that can distort the decisions made on controlling risks.[82] Cost-benefit analyses can get caught up in this interplay and become either cannonballs or cannon fodder within the battle over agency decisions.

The choice of which decisions are subject to analyses and which are not may constitute an abuse. If cost-benefit analysis is such a useful tool, why is it applied more often to regulations that affect industrial activities than to other equally important government decisions. It is argued that this discrimination amounts to using cost-benefit analysis as a political weapon aimed at business' favorite regulatory targets.[83] The same motives have been attributed to federal economic agencies, such as the Council of Economic Advisors and the Council on Wage and Price Stability.[84]

Within the high-stakes game of regulatory poker, there is little trust among the players. Occasional or systematic misuse or abuse of cost-benefit analysis will aggrevate this tension. Whether or not accusations of negligence or intentional fraud are true, this controversy will remain.

The Illinois Experience

Many of the above controversies have occurred in Illinois during its five years of experience with economic impact statements.[85] The Illinois Pollution Control Board has tried to reconcile the economic impact critique and the political nature of its deliberation within one decision-making process, a procedure that some critics give little chance for success[86]. The Board holds at least two public hearings on each economic impact statement at which the preparers are subject to sworn cross-examination by anyone attending the hearing. Since the IINR makes the analyses available prior to the first hearings, opponents and proponents can participate knowledgeably and effectively. Any person may offer additional economic analysis or may rebut the statement in testimony at these hearings.

Problems have arisen, however, from trying to accommodate the state cost-benefit analysis and the dynamic policy-making process of the Pollution Control Board. The analyst is asked to prepare the economic impact statement based on the initial regulatory proposal to the Board. In many important proceedings, this proposal changes many times as a result of negotiations and revisions based on information presented in hearings. Since the Board may promulgate whatever rule it deems important (not just that proposed to it), sometimes the economic impact statement analyzes a proposal greatly different from the regulation established.

The Board also has difficulty knowing what weight to give the economic statements, since it views its mandate as also including political, equity, and ethical issues that must be considered concomitantly with the cost-benefit analysis. The Board receives emotional testimony from concerned community residents that must be factored into its decisions, along with the stark numbers of the economic statement.

Economic impact analyses have been accused of delaying Board decisions.[87] This is somewhat ironic, since many of the regulations proposed since the process was established have been proposed by industry and commercial concerns to relax or adjust standards passed in the early seventies. The economic impact statement process, which these forces convinced the Illinois General Assembly to pass in 1975, has possibly held up these moves to relax pollution controls.

Given the argued potential for misuse or abuse, it is surprising that no such allegations have been made regarding behavior of industrial representatives, environmentalists, or bureaucrats. The number from the statements are seldom if ever misused in unrelated arenas and do not find their way into the media. Of course, this conclusion is based on the observations of a single participant, the author. A more thorough study might reveal more.

Finally, the Illinois experience has not demonstrated too great a difficulty in overcoming the basic philosophical conflict between political processes and scientific policy analysis. The Board and the state EPA appear to be firmly established in a relativistic mode, with the supposed objective analyses merely acting to add more richness to the context from which the decision-making process constructs its versions of truth, reasonableness, feasibility, and equity. For now, the relativists are winning.

Remaining Questions

Many questions remain to be resolved within the political dimension of the cost-benefit analysis controversy:

- Will political decisions of national scope and complexity be able to maintain adequate regard for equity and equitable resource distribution in light of the strong advocacy of cost-benefit analyses?

- While Rodgers argues for "decisive political action"[88] by Congress to produce adequate public health regulations, can Congress or any legislature be asked to make the complex and multitudinous decisions necessary to maintain an environmental protection program?

- What role does or should public participation play in balancing the seeming value neutrality of cost-benefit analysis and in helping agency decision makers to make value judgments in political contexts?[89]

- Can or should current trial-like formal regulatory processes be changed so as to accommodate positivistic economic analyses?

- Should legislatures avoid the problems mentioned above, and many others like them, by establishing more "health only *per se* rules,"[90] which exclude economic considerations from agency decisions?

- Is there something intrinsically different about cost-benefit analyses that separate them from the many other scientific, engineering, biomedical, and statistical analyses used in today's environmental policy decision? If so, what is this quality and what does it indicate about the use of the economic statement?

- Will equity issues ever be so well understood as to allow the quantification necessary to blend them formally into traditional economic analysis?

- Are the two warring critiques discussed by Reich reconcilable?[91] If not, should environmental decision makers explicitly adopt a relativistic or a positivistic approach?

- Are future environmental decisions going to be based more and more on economic factors, or should government agencies adopt Professor Green's attitude that "the methodology of cost-benefit assessment is . . . useful only if it is not taken too seriously?"[92]

ETHICS

It is one thing to learn to use a hammer well. It is quite another to apply this knowledge to a pane of glass. The third major source of controversy over cost-benefit analysis involves whether it is appropriate to apply cost-benefit analysis, skillfully or otherwise, to environmental decisions. Some consider this the fundamental issue.[93] According to Michael Baram, cost-benefit analysis is a "simplistic tool that reduces concern for the individual to a monetized balancing."[94]

There is some confusion as to the nature of the moral question presented by cost-benefit estimates. Ashford, et al., mention the moral issue but do not expand upon it.[95] Freeman exhibits the often-heard response that valuing longevity is merely a question of "how," although he agrees that this question has not been answered well.[96] (In this light, the valuation of human life would be a methodological controversy.) References in the literature to discussions of the moral question are voluminous, yet only a few seek to understand the nature of the controversy.

Laurence Tribe, in an examination of his repugnance toward plastic trees,[97] says that to incorporate values into analytic techniques in the form of human preferences is theoretically possible. However, to believe that this is satisfactory assumes "that the act of characterizing all values as expressions of human preference does not affect their content or distort their perception. It is a premise that does not withstand scrutiny."[98]

Tribe argues that by estimating the worth of a value "attention is no longer directed to the ostensible content of the value, but rather to the fact that it is a more or less abstracted indicium of self-interest."[99] Therefore, the very act of measurement affects the value being measured.

Moral issues enter decision making when the decision maker must choose between alternatives.[100] The decision maker must refer to his or her underlying value function to make this judgment. As the United States moved through the Environmental Decade, pressure built upon the proponents of environmental protection to make more explicit the worth of the values they espoused.[101] Inevitably, this caused a move away from justifying environmentalism as an ethical tenet toward a utilitarian index of the worth of pollution control.[102]

This worth is made explicit and measurable by cost-benefit analysis. Money is used as a "value index" to represent the underlying implicit "function" used to make pollution control decisions. As we relied more heavily on the index and less on the actual function, there was a "loss of meaning."[103] The index of monetized costs and benefits could not capture the totality of the implicit function, e.g., the value of protecting endangered species and pristine wilderness. The decision maker lost some "power of analysis" in this shift.[104] The thesis of the ethics section of this discussion contends that this shift is the true ethical problem with cost-benefit analysis.

Tribe says that this shift causes four distortions.[105] First, analytical techniques collapse process into results, thereby losing the intrinsic value of the process. Second, there is a reduction of wholes and a blending of parts as values are replaced by their "objectively" comparable features. Third, cost-benefit analysis anesthetizes moral feelings by draining terms of their emotional content while striving for objective neutrality. Fourth, the fear of subjectivity limits the role of rationality in decision making by forcing the analyst to ignore his or her own values and forbidding the analyst from asking questions. "Just give me the facts and I'll answer your questions."

What, then, are the values that are particularly susceptible to the reductionist tendencies of cost-benefit analysis? Tribe suggests three categories:[106]

- "Intrinsically incommensurables" such as ecological balance, unspoiled wilderness, species diversity. Once lost, no adequate compensation exists.

- "Inherently global, holistic, or structural features that cannot be reduced to a finite listing" such as urban aesthetics, community cohesion, and, again, ecological balance. Trying to represent the entirety by explicitly valuing the parts loses some value of the whole.

- Values with an "on-off" character, usually with a "deeply evocative and emotional aspect" such as integrity of the body or of the community or of a neighborhood. The reductionism smacks against the value. If it succeeds, the value itself is lost; what remains is a punctured balloon.

In his insightful examination of intuitive negative reactions to economic incentives,[107] Steven Kelman has explored in depth the damage that can be attributed to this reductionism.[108] Although some of the following is drawn from other sources, in the main what follows are his ideas, and the reader will get a better and more complete discussion by referring to Kelman's work in the field.

The use of cost-benefit analysis assumes that polluting behavior can be worthy and can contribute enough to society to be allowed, perhaps even encouraged.[109] This assumption ignores the motive of the behavior. It loses the negative value many care to place on such activity.[110] Kelman argues that society may wish to foster good motives and stigmatize bad ones.[111] By losing that value in the decision calculus, behavior may be allowed that could gradually erode these values, frustrating society's ethical goals.[112]

Similarly, the rational calculatedness of cost-benefit analysis and its emphasis on maximizing self-interest can reduce altruism and spontaneity.[113] Continuous use of economic impact statements reinforces self-interest as a correct or worthy index of value.[114] The praise heaped upon rational decision making implicitly denigrates spontaneity. If society positively values altruism or spontaneity, cost-benefit analysis exacts a social cost.

To the extent that cost-benefit analysis does not deal well with equity considerations, it may cause a similar loss. Kelman maintains that a society may want to "create a domain of equality that consecrates the value of equality."[115] By leaving equity considerations out of the equations, economic analysis may hinder the "development of individual preferences that assign equality a high weight."[116]

Tribe explains that a person may not want a money value placed on air quality (or "breathing rights") because part of the enjoyment of clean air is the knowledge that each person has a right to that air quality *ab initio*.[117]. It is not assigned, nor earned, nor purchased. Constructing a monetized value index for that environmental quality denigrates those rights that are "organically and historically a part of that person rather than assigned on contingent or managerial grounds of efficiency or utility."[118]

A very important part of Kelman's discussion involves the social cost of placing an "instrumental" value on something that used to have an "intrinsic" value.[119] He uses the example of friendship. Friendship is given an intrinsic value by society. It is considered gauche to offer a friend payment for his or her time involved in taking you to the airport. This would imply that you had merely an instrumental value for the friendship. Similarly, gifts of money or of strictly utilitarian goods are less acceptable than thoughtful, intimate, but less expensive presents. Indiscriminately assigning instrumental value changes society's outlook, reinforces negatively valued beliefs, and moves a society toward poor moral positions.[120]

Reducing the intrinsic to the instrumental cheapens the object valued.[121] The specific action of placing a dollar value on human life creates a particularly onerous cost: it eliminates society's ability to hold some things as "not for sale."[122] It makes the adjective "priceless" less meaningful or totally void of content.

Examples of this reductionism are abundant. Note the jarring misfit of using cost-benefit analysis to decide whether to aid a decision to buy a Rembrandt or a Picasso?[123] The residents of Alaska have reduced the value of their state's majesty to mineral wealth. Environmentalists are trying to preserve the value of the country's wild and scenic rivers, its wetlands and its wildlife habitats, while their opponents point to the instrumental value of these areas to commerce and development. This clash between the intrinsic and the instrumental is fundamental to environmental protection.

There is a final cost to consider: the loss of faith in the decisions of the nation's leaders. "This destruction of political legitimacy is perhaps the greatest danger" from the use and abuse of cost-benefit analyses.[124] Today, government decision makers are asked to make their decisions based on a concept of "statistical life." Society may be repulsed by a father selling a child, but when that child's life becomes a statistically derived probability, the government may legitimately act.[125] In his satirical analysis of this ethical nicety, J.G.U. Adams points out the inevitable and rather disturbing end points of such methods.[126]

The public, viewing its leaders making these "objective" distinctions, may begin to lose faith in its system of government. If this alienation continues, "decisions which may seem to be rational from the point of view of a single part of the social system may in fact turn out to be disastrous from the point of view of the continuance of the social system itself."[127]

Thus, far from being an innocent exercise in rationality, cost-benefit analysis may produce social and psychic costs. And therein lies the ethical controversy. Should government agencies use this tool, knowing that the cost of doing so is ethical "dirty hands?"

The Illinois Experience

Kelman's paper attempts to explain the intuitive negative reactions of participants in environmental policy making. This reaction is consistent with the intuitive response of environmentalists in Illinois to the establishment of the economic impact statement requirement. Just as representatives of commerce and industry predicted great things for this new process, so environmentalists felt disaster might befall Illinois' exemplary pollution control system. Neither projection has proved correct.

The shift to a utilitarian rationale for pollution control is evident in Illinois. Currently, air pollution controls are being "balanced" against the need to develop the state's abundant high-sulfur coal reserves. No one seriously speaks of a "right to clean air." Many decry the "losses" in industrial development, productivity, coal use, and capital investment that air quality regulations have "cost" Illinois. Some question whether the state can "afford" any more air pollution control.

So too with bills in the state legislature for wild and scenic rivers and for mandatory deposits on beverage containers. Preserving natural heritage is not as valuable as current usage by riparian owners. The desire to fight the "throwaway mentality" is not nearly as convincing as the dollars and cents of energy savings and employment. In an era of instrumental valuation of natural resources, neither of these laws has passed the Illinois General Assembly. The case for their "worth" has not been made (although a recent economic impact statement on a "bottle bill" regulation should provide some interesting new twists to the discussion).

Whether this attitude of allowing the reduction of intrinsic value to instrumental value is the cause of the cost-benefit program, or whether the program helped foster the attitude, or neither, is an open question requiring more study.

Questions still remain to be resolved in the "ethics" source of controversy:

- Is it true that humans do make implicit life valuations all the time in their daily lives?[128] Or are they exercising some hidden value function that neoclassical economics cannot actually portray on a graph without doing substantial injury to? Can other quantified analyses (other than cost-benefit) be used to adequately represent this process, such as risk assessment or uncertainty analysis? Or is the very act of attempting to be explicit the culprit?[129]

- Can or should society accept the notion of "statistical life?" (Note that if you judge an action by Paretian optimality standards prior to making the decision, the life is "statistical" and therefore an analysis may let you proceed. Judge the action after making the decision, but just before a specific life is lost, and now the specificity raises the cost so near to infinity that the action is no longer justified. No compensation is possible for the loser.) How do the welfare economists respond to J.G.U. Adams' deadly, witty critique?[130]

- If society is going to have to live with some risks, and if resources are limited to control all the risks presented by an industrial age, how should government make the difficult choices as to which risks are acceptable, if quantified analysis is ethically condemned?

- Can analysts develop some new indicator of public good other than "human want satisfaction"?[131]

- How important is it to society to be able to place some things beyond price? John F. Kennedy said in his inaugural address that the U.S. would "pay any price and bear any burden...to assure the survival and the success of liberty." Kelman notes[132] that a significant amount of meaning is lost if Kennedy had said "pay an extremely high and undetermined but finite price and bear an extremely large and undetermined but finite burden...." How important is it to preserve the ability to make that distinction?

CONCLUSION

It is not the purpose of this paper to resolve the controversies over using cost-benefit analysis in environmental regulation.[133] Indeed, it may have raised more thorny issues than it pruned. Instead, this paper has tried to identify three distinct sources of these controversies. The hope is that future discussions will be richer in communication because readers are more aware of the genesis of their attitudes and may be better able to share with one another their arguments, opinions, and feelings about this issue. An evaluation of the success of this endeavor can be conducted by rereading the dialogue with which the paper begins. The reader should be able to assign each statement to its corresponding source. It is hoped that this will shed light on why the two participants in the conversation seem to be saying so much and communicating so little.

Cost-benefit analysis is not a "side-issue" in environmental policy making. Questions of how to analyze data and how to incorporate those data into political decision-making processes are fundamental problems of natural resources management. And at the core of environmentalism in the eighties is the clash between reason and moral perception embodied by the ethical critique of cost-benefit analysis. If environmentalism actually heralds a step toward integrating these two into a new synthesis, a new basis for public decision making,[134] then possibly this paper will help foster the communication necessary to allow environmentalists, industrialists, bureaucrats, and the general public to take that step.

Notes

1. Most of the ideas and actual words in this dialogue are drawn from the literature on cost-benefit analysis. Some of the statements should be familiar to:

Nicholas Ashford, et al. (Benefits of Environmental Health and Safety Regulation, Comm. Print, U.S. Senate, 96th Cong. 2d Sess., March 25, 1980 at 19-20 [hereinafter Ashford, et al.]).

Michael S. Baram (Baram, Cost-Benefit Analysis: An Inadequate Basis for Health, Safety and Environmental Regulatory Decisionmaking, 8 ECOL. L. Q. 473, 484 (1980) [hereinafter An Inadequate Basis]).

Shaul Ben-David, et al. (Ben-David, Kneese and Schulze, A Study of the Ethical Foundations of Benefit-Cost Analysis Techniques, a working paper (August 1979) at 23 [hereinafter Ben-David et al.]).

Kenneth E. Boulding (Boulding, The Ethics of Rational Decision, 12 MANAGEMENT SCIENCES B-161 (1966) [hereinafter Rational Decision]).

Stephen Breyer (Breyer, Analyzing Regulatory Failure: Mismatches, Less Restrictive Alternatives and Reform, 92 HARV. L. REV. 549, 580 (1979) [hereinafter Regulatory Failure]).

Lloyd Cutler and David Johnson (Cutler and Johnson, Regulation and the Political Process, 84 YALE L. J. 1395, 1397 and 1405 (1975) [hereinafter Cutler and Johnson]).

David D. Doniger (Doniger, Federal Regulation of Vinyl Chloride: A Short Course in the Law and Policy of Toxic Substances Control, 7 ECOL. L. Q. 497, 659 (1978) [hereinafter A Short Course]).

A. Myrick Freeman III (A. FREEMAN, THE BENEFITS OF ENVIRONMENTAL IMPROVEMENT: THEORY AND PRACTICE at 5 and 6 (1979) [hereinafter A. FREEMAN]).

J. DeV. Graaf (Graaf, Cost-Benefit Analysis: A Critical View, 43 S. AFRICAN J. OF ECON. 233, 243 (1975)).

Harold P. Green (Green, Cost-Risk Benefit Assessment and the Law: Introduction and Perspective, 45 GEO. WASH. L. REV. 901, 909 (1977) [hereinafter Green]).

Fred Hapgood (Hapgood, Risk-Benefit Analysis—Putting a Price on Life, 243 THE ATLANTIC 33, 36 (January 1979) [hereinafter Hapgood]).

Robert L. Heilbroner (R. L. Heilbroner, THE WORLDLY PHILOSOPHERS [1972]).

Raphael Kasper (Kasper, Cost-Benefit Analysis in Environmental Decision-making, 45 GEO. WASH. L. REV. 1013, 1024 [1977]).

Steven Kelman (Kelman, Economic Incentives and Environmental Policy: Politics, Ideology, and Philosophy, first draft of an as yet unpublished paper, at 80 and 98 [hereinafter Kelman]).

James P. Leape (Leape, Quantitative Risk Assessment in Regulation of Environmental Carcinogens, 4 HARV. ENV. L. REV. 86, 115 [1980]).

Amory Lovins (Lovins, Cost-Risk Benefit Assessments in Energy Policy, 45 GEO. WASH. L. REV. 911, 926 and 920-21 (1977) [hereinafter Lovins]).

John Mendeloff (J. MENDELOFF, REGULATING SAFETY: AN ECONOMIC AND POLITICAL ANALYSIS OF OCCUPATIONAL SAFETY AND HEALTH POLICY at 71 (1979) [hereinafter J. MENDELOFF]).

Thomas H. Moss (Moss, Is There a Scientific Basis for Environmental Decision Making?, presented at Science and Public Policy Colloquium, New York Academy of Sciences, January 3, 1980).

Robert B. Reich (Reich, *Warring Critiques of Regulation*, Regulation 37, 42 (1979) [hereinafter *Warring Critiques*]).

William D. Rowe (Rowe, *Governmental Regulation of Societal Risks*, 45 GEO. WASH. L. REV. 944, 958 (1977) [hereinafter *Societal Risks*]).

Laurence H. Tribe (Tribe, *Ways Not to Think About Plastic Trees: New Foundations for Environmental Law*, 83 YALE L. J. 1315, 1330 (1974) [hereinafter *New Foundations]* and Tribe, *Policy Science: Analysis or Ideology?* 2 PHIL. AND PUB. AFFAIRS 66, 75 (1979) [hereinafter *Analysis or Ideology?*]).

Deborah Lee Williams (Williams, *Benefit-Cost Assessment in Natural Resources Decisionmaking: An Economic and Legal Overview*, 11 NAT. RES. LAW-YER 761, 768 and 785 (1979) [hereinafter Williams]).

2. Cost-benefit analysis can be used by government agencies to decide (1) whether or not to regulate a particular risk and (2) which risks to regulate first. Leape, *Quantitative Risk Assessment in Regulation of Environmental Carcinogens*. 4 HARV. ENV. L. REV. 86, 103-4 (1980). This paper will be addressing the controversies over the first use of cost-benefit analysis.

3. This paper will not review the background and techniques of cost-benefit analysis. The literature is chock full of such discussions. *Cf. Analysis or Ideology?*, *supra* note 1, at 67-75 and A. FREEMAN, *supra* note 1, at 54-59.

4. Ashford, *et al., supra* note 1, at 6.

5. Merrill, *Risk-Benefit Decision-making by the Food and Drug Administration*, 45 GEO. WASH. L. REV. 944 (1977) [hereinafter Merrill]. Valuing human life, according to Merrill, is an institutional or political constraint. *Id.* at 997.

6. Ben-David, *et al., supra* note 1.

7. *See* Ashford, *et al., supra* note 1, at 42. Green and Waitzman mention the moral problem of valuing human life but also do so in the general context of methodology. M. GREEN AND N. WAITZMAN, BUSINESS WAR ON THE LAW: AN ANALYSIS OF THE BENEFITS OF FEDERAL HEALTH/SAFETY ENFORCEMENT at 39 and 41 (1979) [hereinafter BUSINESS WAR].

8. *An Inadequate Basis, supra* note 1, at 489.

9. Ben-David, *et al., supra* note 1.

10. *See* Lovins, *supra* note 1, at 912-17; Ashford, *et al., supra* note 1, at 19; Merrill, *supra* note 5; *A Short Course, supra* note 1, at 519-20; Rodgers, *Benefits, Costs and Risks; Oversight of Health and Environmental Decision-making*, 4 HARV. ENV. L. REV. 191, 193-196 (1980) [hereinafter Rodgers].

11. Rodgers, *supra* note 10, at 197.

12. BUSINESS WAR, *supra* note 7.

13. Ben-David, *et al., supra* note 1, at 8.

14. Ashford, *et al., supra* note 1, at 8.

15. For an authoritative discussion of the work to date and the state-of-the-art, *see* A. Freeman, *The Benefits of Air and Water Pollution Control: A Review and Synthesis of Recent Estimates*, report prepared for the Council on Environmental Quality, December 1979.

16. Lovins, *supra* note 1, at 928-29.

17. Leape, *Quantitative Risk Assessment in Regulation of Environmental Carcinogens*, 4 HARV. ENV. L. REV. 86, 91 (1980). For further discussion of the uncertainties in carcinogenesis, see *A Short Course, supra* note 1, at 508-514.

18. *A Short Course, supra* note 1, at 514-518.

19. Lovins, *supra* note 1, at 925-6, footnote 72.

20. *See Regulatory Failure, supra* note 1, at 572.

21. A. FREEMAN, *supra* note 1, at 249-50.

22. Lovins, *supra* note 1, at 925. For more discussion of data related problems *see A Short Course, supra* note 1, at 516-17.

23. Ashford cautions " 'the analysts' own values are often introduced [when trying to monetize human life] without making clear that this has happened or how their choices affect the result of the analysis." Ashford, *et al., supra* note 1, at 41.

24. *Id.* at 41-42.

25. *Id.* at 41.

26. *An Inadequate Basis, supra* note 1, at 525. *See also* Lovins, *supra* note 1, at 927 and 931.

27. *An Inadequate Basis, supra* note 1, at 489.

28. One could argue that prejudicing the analysis is a political source of controversy, since it constitutes a misuse. *See* text *infra.* However, making honest judgments or assumptions, but failing to indicate these in the analysis is a question of how the work is done; therefore such questions are methodological.

29. *Cf. An Inadequate Basis, supra* note 1, at 491. *See also A Short Course, supra* note 1.

30. *See* text *infra for more discussions on this problem as it occurs in Illinois.*

31. Pursuant to P.L. 79-790 and P.L. 80-1218.

32. Approximately $500,000 per year.

33. *Cf.* MITTELHAUSER, et al. ECONOMIC IMPACT OF CHANGING THE CARBON MONOXIDE EMISSION LIMITATIONS FOR STEEL MILLS, R78-1, IINR Doc. No. 79/14 (June 1979).

34. *See* DONINAR AND ISOE, ECONOMIC IMPACT OF THE CHLORINATION OF PUBLIC WATER SUPPLIES, R78-8, IINR Doc. No. 79/39 (October 1979).

35. *See* YATES, et al., ECONOMIC IMPACT OF INCORPORATING RACT 1 GUIDELINES FOR VOC EMISSIONS INTO THE ILLINOIS AIR POLLUTION CONTROL REGULATIONS, R78-3 and R78-4, IINR Doc. No. 79/01 April 1979.

36. BRIGHAM, *et al.,* ECONOMIC IMPACT OF A SUSPENSION OF RULE 203 AS IT APPLIES TO AN UNNAMED TRIBUTARY OF THE VERMILION RIVER, IINR Doc. No. 80/05, April 1970.

37. *See* ROBERTS AND SIEVERING, A GUIDE TO ENVIRONMENTAL BENEFITS ASSESSMENT IN ECONOMIC IMPACT STUDIES, IINR Doc. No. 77/32 (October 1977).

38. Personal conversation with Irvin Goodman, Vice-Chairman of the Illinois Pollution Control Board.

39. This statement, as is much of the information contained in this section, is based on the author's experience as an environmental public interest attorney practicing before the Pollution Control Board and as the public health representative to the Institute of Natural Resources Economic Technical Advisory Committee, which reviews all economic impact statements and advises the director on the administration of the program.

40. ZERBE, *et al.*, ECONOMIC ANALYSIS OF ENVIRONMENTAL REGULATION IN THE MOTOR RACING INDUSTRY, IINR Doc. No. 76/24, October 1976.

41. During cross-examination before the Board, a mistake made by the consultant was brought out. This figure was recomputed to $648,000. However, it still represents a little over a third of the $1.6 million in benefits estimated by IEPA.

42. The Board ultimately accepted the agency's figures over the contractor's.

43. Rodgers, *supra* note 10, at 193-194.

44. *Cf. An Inadequate Basis, supra* note 1, at 525; A. FREEMAN, *supra* note 1, at 8.

45. Cutler and Johnson, *supra* note 1, at 1405.

46. Williams, *supra* note 1 at 770.

47. Cutler and Johnson, *supra* note 1, at 1402.

48. *Id.*

49. *Warring Critiques, supra* note 1, at 39.

50. *See Analysis or Ideology?, supra* note 1 at 76-8. Tribe argues that this "passion for objectivity" is misplaced.

51. *Cf.* Green, *supra* note 1, at 910.

52. *Regulatory Failure, supra* note 1, at 583-4.

53. Schulz, *The Abrasive Interface* at 18-19, in BUSINESS AND PUBLIC POLICY ed. (John T. Dunlop, 1980).

54. Ashford, *et al., supra* note 1, at 43.

55. Hapgood uses the example of devising an "efficient" Pap smear program. It costs less per life saved, but more women are at risk. Unless the savings are used to compensate the women, they are paying with their health for savings which benefit others. Hapgood, *supra* note 1, at 35.

56. *See* A. FREEMAN, *supra* note 1, at 262-3; Williams, *supra* note 1, at 770-2; BUSINESS WAR, *supra* note 7, at 61-2; Kasper, *Cost-Benefit Analysis in Environmental Decisionmaking*, 45 GEO. WASH. L. REV. 1013, 1021 (1977).

57. *See An Inadequate Basis, supra* note 1, at 488-9. See Ben-David, *et al., supra* note 1, at 32.

58. *See generally* Ben-David, *et al., supra* note 1. Their table (at page 39) shows how the discount rate is associated with the ethical posture that is chosen for determining equity between intergenerational populations. The case studies illustrate that what the authors call "ethical" considerations are actually distributional (and therefore political) questions.

59. *A Short Course, supra* note 1, at 676.

60. *See Regulatory Failure, supra* note 1, at 570. Doniger's impressive case study is an excellent documentation of the political issues involved in these decisions. *See A Short Course, supra* note 1, at 563-565 and 585-88.

61. Merrill, *supra* note 5, at 1001.

62. Green, *supra* note 1, at 904.

63. *Cf. Regulatory Failure, supra* note 1, at 575.

64. Rowe points out that humans are more concerned with adverse consequences than with the benefits of risk-taking. *Societal Risks, supra* note 1, at 960.

Lovins argues that democratic processes work well if they implement this preference. Lovins, *supra* note 1, at 943.

65. Lovins, *supra* note 1, at 940.

66. *Id.* Cutler and Johnson suggest that things have gone too far, that current
methods of agency decision making have erected barriers to possible impacts by
politically accountable officials. Cutler and Johnson, *supra* note 1, at 1403.

67. Rowe argues for a four step process of determining "risk acceptability":
1. Direct gain-loss analysis
2. Indirect gain-loss analysis
3. Cost-effectiveness of risk reduction alternatives
4. Reconciliation of risk inequities.

Societal Risks, supra note 1, at 961.

68. Rowe would replace his process for "fallible" subjective decision making.
However, he says that number four is the "most important step." He says that this
action should be based on "risk references" determined from previous decisions.
But those previous decisions included a large dose of subjectivity. If prior subjective decisions produced preferences valid enough to use in current decisions, why
not employ the subjective methods used before? *See id.* at 962-3.

69. *Rational Decision, supra* note 1, at B-167. Tribe makes a similar point,
that the "objective" analyst is not supposed to phrase the questions, merely answer
those that the decision maker poses. Tribe argues that this limiting of the inquiry is
a distortion due to the emphasis on objectivity in policy sciences. *Analysis or Ideology?, supra* note 1, at 102-5.

70. *An Inadequate Basis, supra* note 1, at 502-15. However, setting priorities
subjectively (i.e., politically) runs the risk of locking out minorities and other pow-
erless members of society. Hapgood, *supra* note 1, at 37.

71. *Regulatory Failure, supra* note 1, at 574.

72. Lovins, *supra* note 1, at 939-43. According to Baram consideration of hu-
manistic and environmental principles is "incompatible with a regulatory decision-
making process in which economic factors play a dominant role." *An Inadequate
Basis, supra* note 1, at 524.

73. Rodgers, *supra* note 10, at 201-14.

74. *Id.* at 214-219. *See generally A Short Course, supra* note 1, at 654-76.

75. *See* Rodgers, *supra* note 10, at 219-225; *A Short Course, supra* note 1, at
664-67. Lovins says that much of the decisions society faces involve "transscientific" issues. Then the matter becomes a question of decision rules. Does society require people to prove risk or safety, acceptability or unacceptability of risk?
Does society want proof or mere engineering judgment? Lovins, *supra* note 1, at
920-21.

76. *See* Rodgers, *supra* note 10, at 200-1.

77. Reich predicts that when the costs of regulation fall on a small group and
the benefits are widespread, there will be a strong push for economic assessment.
This is true of current health and safety regulations. But when the costs of regulation are spread out and the benefits accrue to a concentrated population, then the
political responsiveness critique would be expected to win out. This is the case with
cartel regulation. *Warring Critiques, supra* note 1, at 42.

78. Ruttenberg, *An Overview of the Issues and A Framework for Analyzing
Them,* presented at Regulatory Controversy: The Case for Health and Safety, conference held in Washington, D.C. on March 7 and 8, 1980.

79. Lovins, *supra* note 1, at 939-40.

80. A. FREEMAN, *supra* note 1.

81. *Id.* at 1.

82. *See* J. MENDELOFF, *supra* note 1, at 79.

83. From a conversation between Richard Liroff of The Conservation Foundation and David Doniger. *See generally,* BUSINESS WAR, *supra* note 7.

84. *An Inadequate Basis, supra* note 1, at 509-15.

85. Again, this section is based largely on the author's professional experiences.

86. *Warring Critiques, supra* note 1, at 42.

87. The additional two hearings held solely on economic matters are responsible for the bulk of the delay. One lawyer who represents public utilities and other industrial clients before the Pollution Control Board also told the author that this delay becomes important when he advises his clients as to whether or not they should pursue a rule change in front of the Board. (Incidentally, he also pointed out the trade secret problems and anti-trust liability that might arise from a petitioner industry trying to get from competitors the costs data necessary to make their case.) *Cf. Rodgers, supra* note 10, at 200.

88. Rodgers, *supra* note 10, at 204.

89. Ashford, *et al.*, suggest that cost-benefit analyses should be done, if at all, more pluralistically, with more communication between more people representing more disciplines. Ashford, *et al., supra* note 1, at 42. The author is currently exploring the possibilities of using public participation as a mechanism for informing government decision makers as to the values which the public holds and as an indication of the extent to which the public would like government to act to implement those values. *See also* Merrill, *supra* note 5, at 1011-12.

90. For more discussion of this question, *see A Short Course, supra* note 1, at 656-57.

91. *Cf. Warring Critiques, supra* note 1, at 41-2.

92. Green, *supra* note 1, at 910.

93. *See An Inadequate Basis, supra* note 1, at 485.

94. *Id.* at 524.

95. Ashford, *et al., supra* note 1, at 18.

96. A. FREEMAN, *supra* note 1, at 249.

97. *New Foundations, supra* note 1.

98. *Id.* at 1329.

99. *Id.* Kelman illustrates this problem with the absurd extension of valuing sex by looking at how much people pay for prostitutes. Kelman, *supra* note 1, at 120-121. *See also* Williams, *supra* note 1, at 788.

100. *Rational Decision, supra* note 1, at B-162.

101. See generally *New Foundations, supra* note 1.

102. Ben-David, *et al.*, show that strict utilitarianism is not the basis of cost-benefit analysis. They produce a counterinstance where utilitarianism would compel one action, while a cost-benefit analysis would indicate a second action. Ben-David, *et al., supra* note 1, at 12. They also indicate that most of the "moral" (i.e.,

distributional) arguments against cost-benefit analysis are founded in a Liberatarian or a Rawlsian ethic. *Id.* at 32.

103. Meaning is used here in its epistemological sense, having a content of knowledge. The figure below may help illustrate:

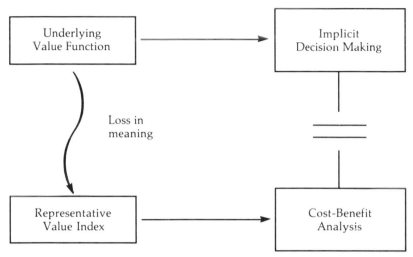

The loss in meaning that comes from representing the underlying actual value function by a convenient index leads to the disparity between the intuitive decision making and the results of a cost-benefit analysis. Cost-benefit analysis therefore bcomes an imperfect representation of the individual decision process. To the extent that the value index replaces the underlying function, the cost-benefit work replaces imperfectly and incorrectly the actual decisions that might be made. *See Rational Decision, supra* note 1, at B-165.

104. Power is used in a statistical sense, the ability of a test to discern correctly all important distinctions. A less powerful analysis will fog important distinctions, thereby leading to poorer decisions. The lessening of power is a result of the loss in information. Tribe calls this loss a "reduction." *New Foundations, supra* note 1, at 1331. For an examination of the philosophical roots of this reductionism *see id.* at 1332-36.

105. *Analysis or Ideology? supra* note 1, at 79-105.

106. *Id.* at 96. Rodgers has tried a similar classification. Rodgers, *supra* note 10, at 194-195.

107. Kelman, *supra* note 1.

108. He identifies four ethical questions:

1. Should we care about motives?
2. Should we care about statements implicit within control strategies chosen?
3. Should equity be considered in program design?
4. Should we keep currently unpriced things from being priced?

Id. at 69-70.

109. Governor James Thompson of Illinois has repeatedly stated his accept-

ance of "dirtier air" if it would lead to more development and use of the state's abundant coal reserves.

110. For examples of this loss, *see* Kelman, *supra* note 1, at 71-2 and *Analysis or Ideology?, supra* note 1, at 1339. This is an example of Tribe's "process reduction."

111. For examples and further discussion *see* Kelman, *supra* note 1, at 74, 76 and 87-8.

112. "To most people, a moral condemnation of fraud or other crime is important and the statement that some level other than zero is optimal counteracts that necessary moral condemnation." *Id.* at 86.

113. *Id.* at 77-81 and 83-88

114. Mendeloff notes that if people derive satisfaction from thinking of themselves as altruists, and if such values are widely held "then rational action may require that collective decisions eschew the guidelines that economic analysis provides. In other words, people may be willing to give up some material benefits in exchange for the psychic benefits of satisfying criteria they value more." J. MENDELOFF, *supra* note 1.

115. Kelman, *supra* note 1, at 90.

116. *Id.* at 91.

117. *Analysis or Ideology?, supra* note 1, at 88-9.

118. Lovins, *supra* note 1, at 929.

119. Kelman, *supra* note 1, at 103 and 106-7. *See also New Foundations, supra* note 1, at 1332.

120. *New Foundations, supra* note 1, at 1347.

121. Kelman, *supra* note 1, at 118.

122. *Id.* at 121-123.

123. *Analysis or Ideology?, supra* note 1, at 84.

124. Lovins, *supra* note 1, at 939-40.

125. Kelman, *supra* note 1, at 96-7.

126. Adams takes two premises from Mishan's work (that people will pay more to avoid risk to an unknown person than to a specifically identified person and that small risks cost exponentially less than large risks) and follows them to the conclusion that projects which assign small risks randomly to very large numbers of people should be favored. Adams, . . . *and How Much for your Grandmother?* 6 ENVIRONMENTAL AND PLANNING A 619 (1974) [hereinafter Adams]. The absurdity of his conclusions and their likelihood for conflict with the public's intuitive reactions point out the danger of negative public reaction to decisions based on the cost-benefit logic.

127. *Rational Decision, supra* note 1, at B-166. Boulding calls this a "principle of very great importance." Lovins expresses similar fears. Lovins, *supra* note 1, at 916.

128. *See* A. FREEMAN, *supra* note 1, at 6 and 166.

129. Can decision makers avoid the trap of allowing the implicit and more important underlying value function to be replaced by the explicit value index chosen to represent it?

130. Or do those commentators who have cited Adams' work agree with his arguments in favor of exploring "economies of ignorance." Adams, *supra* note 126, at 623.

131. *See New Foundations, supra* note 1, at 1332.

132. Kelman, *supra* note 1, at 128.

133. Baram suggests some "pragmatic" and "incremental" changes that might be implemented. *An Inadequate Basis, supra* note 1, at 525-529. *See generally* Williams, *supra* note 1; *A Short Course, supra* note 1; Rodgers, *supra* note 10.

134. *New Foundations, supra* note 1, at 1336.

5/METHODS

Benefit-Cost Analysis and the Common Sense of Environmental Policy*

Arthur P. Hurter, Jr., George S. Tolley, and Robert G. Fabian

Much of the controversy over environmental policies can be attributed to the fact that some people emphasize the benefits and minimize the disadvantages of a particular policy while others do just the opposite. Although this is due partly to a difference in priorities and values, it is also due partly to the problems involved in determining advantages and disadvantages, a process that requires expertise from many diverse fields. For example, the knowledge of physicians and epidemiologists is essential for collecting information on health effects of pollution. Similarly, engineering knowledge is essential in the design of environmental control measures.

Some parts of this chapter contain material from Environmental Policy: Elements of Environmental Analysis, Vol. 1. Edited by George S. Tolley, Philip E. Graves, and Glenn C. Blomquist. (Copyright 1981 by Ballinger Publishing Company). Reprinted with permission.

* We have been asked to comment on why we prefer the word ordering "benefit-cost" in our chapter. About 25 years ago, serious interest among professional economists initiated a literature in the field concerned with estimating benefits and costs of natural resource projects, drawing on concepts out of the mainstream of economics. This literature is referred to as the literature on benefit-cost analysis, which is the first reason for preferring the word ordering we use. An earlier, largely engineering literature is suggested by the term "cost-benefit" analysis. That earlier literature was more mechanistic, less systematic, and less concerned with the difficult frontier issues.

The second reason for preferring the word ordering is that difficult issues in benefit-cost analysis concern benefits, not costs. If the word costs is placed first, the emphasis is wrong.

The third reason is that, when ratios are used in comparing projects, the ratio used is the ratio of benefits to costs, not costs to benefits. The higher the benefit-

Once the effects of an environmental regulation have been estimated, a crucial problem remains: how can the various effects of a
regulation be compared with one another? What kind of framework can be used to compare the improved health of residents in a
cleaned-up area with the increased cost of goods and services? In
this essay, we first discuss the type of framework that can be used to
compare the various effects of environmental regulations. We then
proceed to a discussion of the potential sources of uncertainty in assessing both the benefits and the costs of environemtnal regulations. In the concluding section of the essay, we offer strategies to
help decision makers make better use of cost-benefit analysis in assessing environmental policies.

AGREEING ON A FRAMEWORK

Economic analysis is one tool or framework that can be used to
compare the various effects of environmental regulations. But
many object to the use of economic analysis, stating that various effects of environmental actions are noncommensurate and conse-
quently should not be compared. When formulating environmental
policy, however, these effects must be compared either explicitly or
implicitly. In fact, comparison of seemingly noncommensurate
things is not only common but inevitable. For example, everyday
decisions involve comparing such seemingly noncommensurate
items as the nutritional value and culinary delight of food with increased self-confidence and social advancement associated with being thin and wearing stylish clothing. Weighing such trade-offs is
inevitable as long as there is more than one commodity people wish
to consume.

---

cost ratio, the more preferred the project, other things being equal. The ordering
benefit-cost suggests that benefit-cost ratios are relevant, not the more contorted
concept of a cost-benefit ratio, which would vary inversely with how preferred a
project is.

A fourth reason for preferring the word ordering, perhaps less important but
still not to be ignored, is that placing the word costs first seems to suggest a negative attitude toward projects, as if this type of analysis is designed to pose a barrier
to projects. Economic concepts, particularly as reflected in benefit-cost analysis,
are of course completely neutral toward the undertaking of projects. The primary
purpose of using these concepts is precisely to introduce objectivity. Too often, we
feel, there are attempts to portray benefit-cost analysis in a negative way.

These trade-offs, made by individuals in personal decisions, also are made in group or public decisions, for example, in decisions formulating environmental policy. Thus, when considering actions to control environmental pollution, advantages must be weighed against disadvantages and trade-offs between apparently noncommensurate items must be made.

The problem of estimating weights for different, seemingly incomparable effects requires going beyond qualitative into quantitative assessment. If only one effect were important, then analysis could be limited to a qualitative comparison of this single dimension, for example, human health. But when considering alternative environmental policies with varying costs, analyzing only a single dimension is inadequate and potentially misleading. For example, one action that may only minimally improve the environment and human health could be considered desirable because its costs would be relatively small. Another action that may be expected to produce sizable improvements could be considered undesirable because its costs would be relatively large.

As seen above, creating sound environmental policy requires two related steps: (1) establishing a framework for making comparisons, and (2) making quantitative estimates within that framework. The framework suggested by economists—benefit-cost analysis—although used to some extent, is not universally accepted for a variety of reasons. One reason is that the quantitative estimates have been suspect, a problem occasionally exacerbated by the practice of according results a numerical precision that is not justified. Particularly troublesome can be the instances in which a single number representing benefits is compared with a single number representing costs without any recognition of the uncertainty that may surround both. However, this criticism of benefit-cost analysis has been overdone. In many and perhaps most cases, either the benefits exceed the costs by a wide margin or vice versa. In these cases, the ranges or outcomes are not large enough to affect the comparison appreciably.

Partial frameworks, which concentrate only on the benefits of improving the environment or only on the disadvantages or costs of controlling pollution, sometimes have been used. Typically these frameworks have focused on the physical effects of pollution without making the different types of effects comparable enough to consider the trade-offs among them. Because using such frameworks often implies that estimates are more precise than they actually are, these frameworks provide an unbalanced view of the totality of effects and are of limited use to a decision maker genuinely concerned with weighing all the effects.

Measurement Problems

When comparing the effects of any environmental policy, two types of uncertainty or error may be distinguished. One is error in estimating physical effects, e.g., the improvement in human health associated with cleaner air. The second is error in estimating the weights to be attached to the physical effects, for example, the weights, often expressed in dollars, associated with an improvement in human health. A common view is that the estimates of physical effects, determined by physical scientists, are "hard" evidence and are inherently more accurate than are the "soft" estimates of human behavior made by economists or other social scientists. As the formulation of environmental policy grows more sophisticated and as the uncertainty involved in estimation is examined more extensively, it may well become apparent that the estimates from social scientists are "harder" than the scientific evidence of the physical effects of pollution. For instance, although it is difficult to determine how much "less sickness" is worth, the range of uncertainty about this economic question is far less than the uncertainty concerning the physical effects of air pollution on sickness.

Establishing Trade-Offs

The weights attached to the physical effects of an environmental policy specify the trade-offs that people are willing to make between one physical effect and another. But who should make the comparisons? Whose trade-offs should be considered? The relevant trade-offs should be those made by the people affected by the environmental policy. Accordingly, the weights on the benefits of an environmental policy are the trade-offs that the people affected are willing to make between a cleaner environment and other goals. Similarly, the weights on the costs of producing a cleaner environment are the trade-offs that the people incurring the costs are willing to make.

It is important to clarify whose trade-offs are being considered, since some discussions imply that trade-offs by those other than the individuals affected are relevant to a decision. For example, some suggest that the trade-offs should be made by a policy maker or by some wise person other than those affected by the particular policy. In our view, the opinions of a journalist in Boston who feels that the carbon monoxide content of the air should be lower in St. Louis should be of little interest to the decision maker concerned with the trade-offs that the people in St. Louis are willing to make. The relevant trade-offs are those of the people receiving the consequent advantages and disadvantages of an environmental policy.

It is also important to consider the distribution of income and so-called distributional weights. These weights indicate the value to be assigned to the welfare of those bearing benefits and costs and should be distinguished from the comparisons of environmental quality and other valuable factors. To date, economic analysis has contributed relatively little on distributional weights. The customary assumption is that economics can contribute to increasing the total amount of satisfaction in society by estimating the trade-offs among different types of effects. How that satisfaction should be distributed among people with different incomes has not been studied extensively.

Economic analysis can contribute substantially to estimating the distributional impact of environmental actions without assigning weights to the various people affected. It should be noted in this regard that long-term costs and advantages can not only differ greatly from short-term effects but are determined partly by people's responsiveness to the short-term impacts.

Convenience of Measuring in Dollars

Economists usually express weights, whether they represent trade-offs of different physical effects or of distributional effects, in dollar terms. This practice has been labeled as shallow, incomplete, and callous and has produced a tendency, in some forums, to attempt to preclude economics from the formulation of environmental policy. Such a view reflects a lack of understanding about the criteria used to make choices.

When weights are given in dollar terms, it does not imply that it is the dollars themselves that matter; dollars merely are a convenient unit in which to express people's trade-offs. Units other than dollars can be used to express weights or trade-offs. The use of clams, oil, or miles of visibility instead of dollars would make inescapable the fact that people are willing to give up one worthwhile thing for another; it can be difficult, however, to make comparisons when different units are used simultaneously.

The justifiable concern that the environment may be neglected in private decisions suggests that there are crucial trade-offs worthwhile to make through public policy. However, this concern does not justify the naive position that environmental action to abate pollution should be taken without weighing advantages and disadvantages. It is clear that the value of numerous aspects of the environment is far less than infinite. Few people would choose to live in burlap forever to get five more miles of visibility; similarly few people would exist at starvation levels to get pure water. Given this, expressing weights in dollar terms is an integral part of making environmental decisions in a way most beneficial to all society.

SOURCES OF UNCERTAINTY

Having discussed the framework that can be used to compare the benefits and costs of environmental programs and regulations, we proceed to a discussion of the potential sources of uncertainty, bias, and error in assessing these benefits and costs. We detail these sources of uncertainty to help decision makers reduce these shortcomings and to help them interpret the results of benefit-cost analysis performed with currently available methods and data.

Benefits, Costs, and Market Prices

Benefits and costs would be relatively easy to measure if they were the result of transactions that indicated clearly individuals' willingness to pay for marketed goods. But since public goods such as national defense or clean air are not traded in a marketplace, the analyst must infer the affected individuals' willingness to pay for them. For example, the aesthetic quality of a clean lake can be assigned a monetary value, but the procedures necessary for such a valuation are indirect. Economic theory is a useful guide to benefit estimation primarily because it provides ways of measuring willingness to pay when market information is unavailable. Private benefits from government actions usually are evaluated using the market prices for the flow of goods and services from a specific project or the changes in these flows associated with a particular regulation. Market prices do not always convey accurate information about willingness to pay, however, because of market distortions.

Private costs ordinarily are measured in terms of the monetary expenditure required to undertake a project or respond to a regulation. Underlying this measure is the idea that economic cost is the value of opportunities foregone (opportunity cost). For example, assuming full employment, undertaking a pollution control project requires that labor and materials be diverted from other uses, thus resulting in diminished production and consumption elsewhere in the economy. The value of these foregone opportunities is the cost of the pollution control program. Just as in the case of benefits, not all costs are measured accurately by prices that result from market transactions. For example, when those unemployed are hired to work on a project, and they are paid a wage greater than the minimum required to attract them to the project (their supply price), only the supply price should be counted as project cost; any wage payment greater than supply price is simply a transfer of project benefits to labor. This estimation of supply price is referred to in economic literature as shadow pricing.

Private benefits and costs, while registered in the marketplace, do not always accurately reflect the willingness to pay of individuals. Markets may be distorted in various ways, causing prices to reflect individual valuations inaccurately. Taxes are an important example of a market distortion that the analyst must consider carefully in benefit-cost analysis. Product or productive input pricing, which reflects the presence of monopoly, is also relevant. In addition, the distinction between monetary outlays and the true opportunity costs must be considered by the benefit-cost analyst. For example, suppose that an environmental project requires the purchase of cement, which is subject to a sales tax. The supply price of cement, which is the social cost or opportunity cost to society of the cement, is the net-of-tax price of the cement. The tax receipts resulting from purchase of the cement for the project are part of project benefits transferred to the tax collector.

In addition to taking account of market distortions, the benefit-cost analyst must consider the effects of a project on prices in various markets affected by the project. For example, if purchases of cement are expected to raise its price, the analyst must attempt to forecast the extent to which cement prices will rise and include these expected price increases in the costs of the project. Failure to anticipate the price increase would cause an underestimate of project cost. By using supply and demand analysis together with actual data on the cement industry, the analyst can calculate the project cost correctly.

The benefit-cost analyst also must look beyond the direct effects of increased cement costs. If the increased cost of cement confers net benefits or costs on other sectors of the economy, these net benefits or costs must be included in the calculation of project benefits and costs, even if these sectors are unrelated to the project. The presence of market distortions in the other markets is of particular importance here since all benefits and costs of the project, direct and indirect, must be included in the analysis. This is because benefit-cost analysis is carried out from a social perspective, in which all members of society are taken into account.

Real Benefits and Distributional Effects

When conducting benefit-cost analysis, real benefits should be distinguished from distributional effects. Real benefits are those effects of a project characterized by increases in satisfaction and/or decreases in the total amount of resources required to produce goods and services. For example, the real benefits of increased water quality may be approximated by the amount people are willing to pay for the additional enjoyment of fishing, swimming, and boating. Distributional effects are changes that occur in the well-being of one group of individuals at the expense of another group. For example, increased fishing due to improved water quality might increase the price of fishing equipment, thus increasing the profit of the merchants. Improved water quality might also result in increased motel facilities. If there were relatively full employment, any resources used for motel construction would have to be diverted from other productive activities. These effects are transfers from one set of purchasers and sellers to another, rather than increases in productive activity. They are not project benefits, although one group or region might benefit at the expense of another. Benefit-cost analysis should include the real benefits but not the distributional effects.

Estimating Costs

Three basic approaches for estimating the costs of pollution control strategies are often used: (1) the survey technique, (2) engineering estimation, and (3) statistical estimation. The *survey method* relies on the polluter to provide information on emissions and control costs and assumes that the respondent is both knowledgeable and honest. The *engineering approach* relies extensively on technical analysis for cost estimates. Knowledge of the type and quantity of outputs as well as the underlying technical processes enables the analyst to estimate both uncontrolled pollutant levels and expenditures relating to the most efficient (least cost) methods of achieving various target levels of control. The analyst must assume that the polluter uses a "typical" production technology, must determine the control strategy being used, and then must estimate current emission levels. The analyst must forecast the method that the polluter will choose to attain further control levels and then must estimate the cost of the selected technology. This approach is likely to be very costly and requires the analyst to have an adequate level of technological expertise. The *statistical approach* requires that the analyst use statistical methods to discover the specific relationship between inputs and output. Cost functions then are derived from the statistical "production function." A limitation of the statistical approach is that once new control techniques are developed, adequate historical data for a statistical analysis are not likely to exist.

There are several problems with these methods for estimating costs. For example, the analyst frequently is required to estimate the cost of reducing specific pollutants. Since control procedures tend to alter emissions of several pollutants simultaneously, it is often difficult to determine the cost of reducing a particular pollutant. The analyst should explain this problem if required to make arbitrary cost allocations.

Another problem is that the cost estimates generally are derived on an industry-by-industry basis. But industry designation follows the Standard Industrial Classification system, which is based on product classification. These classifications may not be appropriate for pollution control cost aggregations. For example, it would be more feasible to measure the costs and benefits of cleaning up sulfur dioxide emissions than to measure the costs of cleaning up the "stone, clay and glass" industry. Groupings according to sulfur dioxide emissions and available control technologies may be a more appropriate basis for cost estimate aggregation than groupings based on industrial products. It is important that the benefit-cost analyst carefully consider the most appropriate approach to aggregation at the beginning of a study.

A third problem stems from not adequately considering the interdependency among firms in choosing pollution control techniques. A common method of assessing the costs of a pollution control program is to determine the cost of each of the separate control activities that reduces pollution and then add these costs together to obtain the total program costs. Although there are usually several possible control alternatives for each firm or source of pollution, it is reasonable to assume that the firm will choose the least costly response to program requirements. If the choice of one firm is independent of the choices of other firms, then the least cost response will be relatively easy to predict. Many of these choices, however, are not independent. For example, if firm B is downstream of firm A, the alternatives available to B will depend on the strategy selected by A. In other words, the least costly response for one firm might depend on the control strategies chosen by other firms. The overall estimation of program cost typically is complicated by such consideration of interdependence. These considerations underscore the need for the analyst to think through the long-run effects of a project or regulation.

Property Value Estimates of Benefits and Costs

The attractiveness of an area as a place of residence or business is determined by many characteristics, one of which is the quality of the physical environment. Two residential areas, equally attractive in other respects, would be expected to differ in value if the environment of one were polluted and the other clean. Identical houses in each of the areas would command different prices. These price differences would reflect the prospective resident's valuation of anticipated occupancy of the two houses.

The relationship between property values and environmental quality provides the benefit-cost analyst with a market in which willingness to pay for environmental quality is registered in terms of prices. Although, for example, house prices do not measure the value of environmental quality directly they can, through appropriate statistical techniques, be used to measure the value of environmental quality to residents of the area.

The property-value method of estimating the benefits of environmental improvement has two components: (1) a statistical study of the relationship between property values and environmental quality, and (2) a determination of the effect of a project or regulation on the level of pollution. Combining the two steps provides a dollar measure of project benefits.

There is a growing amount of literature on the property-value method, addressing some important technical and statistical problems associated with the method's use. For example, the fact that some individuals have greater aversion to pollution than others complicates the measurement of willingness to pay for environmental improvement. The analyst also should take account of the various expenditures people make to protect themselves against a polluted environment. A pollution control project or regulation would reduce some of these expenditures. For example, less frequent house painting and cleaning might be required; fewer air conditioners might be purchased, or they might be operated for shorter periods of time. Some cost savings take the form of rearranging daily schedules to engage in more desirable activities; time might be saved which was previously devoted to pollution avoidance. Since no market exists in these activities, they would have to be shadow priced. It is unlikely that property value differences would reflect all of these benefits from pollution reduction. It is up to the benefit-cost analyst to make judgments about them, perhaps by incorporating them in an economic model of response to environmental improvement.

Survey Methods

Benefits and costs usually can be measured by using market prices of goods, services, and productive inputs. Sometimes market prices must be adjusted for distortions such as taxes or monopoly influences. Sometimes the market provides prices only indirectly indicative of willingness to pay; for example, property value differentials as a measure of pollution damage. In all of these uses of price, the market is yielding information about people's valuations based on actual decisions they have made. Occasionally, however, benefit-cost analysts use questionnaire surveys to get direct information on willingness to pay.

Questionnaire surveys must be designed to elicit information as accurately as possible. Questions must be expressed in a way that avoids leading the respondent in a particular direction. It is especially important to structure a questionnaire situation so that the respondent is able to focus on the issues clearly. Extraneous influences, such as the tendency for a respondent to give the answer he or she thinks the interviewer desires, need to be avoided. Ideally, questionnaire surveys should be used to corroborate market information, in which preferences are revealed through actual decisions.

Even the most skillfully designed survey, however, cannot create a situation in which the respondent can make a genuine willingness-to-pay decision.

Option Value and Irreversible Decisions

Measured willingness to pay for the benefits of a project or regulation is likely to underestimate the true benefits of a project when the future demand for some related product is uncertain. For example, consider additional or better recreational facilities. Suppose that if the project or regulation is not undertaken now, it will be impossible to provide these facilities at a later date. Thus, the current decision is irreversible. Under these circumstances, the benefits of the project or regulation can be separated into two parts: (1) the present and future benefits to those who are certain to use the facility, and (2) the benefits to those who are not sure they will use the facility but who support its establishment because they feel it is important to keep their options and those of future generations open. This second class of benefits, often called "option values" is potentially important when irreversibility exists and is not fully captured by the usual willingness-to-pay measures.

Discounting Benefits and Costs to Present Value

The effects of environmental projects and regulations extend many years into the future. For any given project, the time profile of benefits is likely to differ from the time profile of costs; frequently costs are concentrated in the near future while significant benefits do not appear for a number of years. In addition, different projects, perhaps competing for scarce resources for environmental improvement, have different time profiles of benefits. In order to compare the expected effects of various regulations over time, the anticipated costs and benefits must be discounted to present value. For example, $1,000 of costs imposed by a project 10 years from now will be valued less than $1,000 of costs that must be borne immediately. How much to discount deferred costs and benefits is a problem the analyst must solve in order to evaluate and compare projects. Once a discount rate has been determined, the analyst can calculate the net present value of projects, and costs and benefits can be compared in terms of these equivalent values to society today. The net present value of projects is sensitive to the value of the discount rate. Analysts frequently employ alternative discount rates to establish a range of measures of benefits and costs.

Professional and Political Bias

In view of the uncertainty surrounding the measurement of costs and benefits, subjectivity can color analyses. Unconsciously, the personal biases of an investigator may creep in. Within any agency, unconscious pressures exist for an analyst to make assumptions favorable to the agency's purpose. In political forums, there can be a tendency to take advocacy positions wherein the name of the game is to deliberately choose assumptions as favorable as possible to one's position. The analyst must resist such pressures, however subtly they may be manifested. The influences can sometimes be countered by having analyses conducted by agencies or organizations with conflicting vested interests or viewpoints.

STRATEGIES FOR AIDING DECISION MAKERS

Given the unavoidable existence of some uncertainty, error, and bias—even if the best efforts are made to eliminate them—can adequate procedures be devised for dealing with these factors? The answer to this is complex and provides the grist for further work aimed at improved public decision making. If the consequences of environmental actions are to be compared systematically, the issue is not whether to undertake benefit-cost analysis but rather how to make it as useful as possible. Efforts must be allocated intelligently, results must not appear more precise than they actually are, and decision makers must be given a basis for understanding the results so that they can evaluate them thoughtfully. We offer the following suggestions for meeting these challenges.

Analyze Several Alternatives

To provide decision makers with sufficient information to analyze a proposal, a number of policy alternatives should be assessed. Policy alternatives are defined here as a collection of assumptions about the nature of a regulation. These include factors such as the stringency of the regulation, its comprehensiveness, and its compliance schedule.

How many policy alternatives should be analyzed? One viewpoint is simply to evaluate the benefits and costs of the proposed regulation. If the proposal is altered during the public-decision process, then these alterations would have to be evaluated at a later date or in a different set of hearings.

A second procedure is to evaluate both the proposed regulation and minor modifications of it in order to assess the effect that small changes would have on the costs and benefits of the regulation. For example, if a maximum lead standard were proposed at X parts per million, analysts could consider the costs and benefits of the proposal, together with the costs and benefits of hypothetical proposals that set the standard at 90 percent and at 110 percent of the proposed standard.

A third option is to assess the proposed regulation and one "challenger" proposal developed after discussions with groups likely to oppose the proposed regulation. Thus, if the Environmental Protection Agency proposes a lead standard at X parts per million, industrial groups may help develop a challenger proposal involving a standard of Y parts per million that may find much greater acceptance in industrial circles. The evaluation of the original proposal and one challenger would tend to crystallize those issues that would be brought before a pollution control board during formal hearings on the proposal.

A fourth option is to evaluate a broad range of proposals in order to generate a benefit-cost relation showing the effect of wide variations in the stringency of the proposed regulation. Such an approach implicitly assumes that policy makers will not only assess small changes to the regulation or changes proposed by groups having challenging positions but also may take the initiative in making and promulgating a regulation that is significantly different from the one proposed.

The choice among these alternatives will depend upon the situation and context of the particular proposal being made. The cost of the analysis will increase, of course, as the range of alternative proposals being evaluated increases. The analyst should have a clear understanding in the initial stages of the investigation about the extent of the regulatory alternatives to be evaluated.

Choose Aggregation Carefully

The level of aggregation used to assess benefits and costs varies widely, depending partly on the factors being studied and the objectives of the assessment. If a regulation affects relatively few emission sources, then the analyst may decide to do a very detailed study of each pollution source in order to determine compliance behavior and control costs. An example of this would be a sulfur dioxide regulation that affects only major power plants outside metropolitan areas. Because relatively few sources are affected and because each source may incur a significant control cost, the analyst is justified in extensively examining each generating plant. In other cases, such as the control of hydrocarbon sources, thousands of individual pollution control sources may be involved. In such cases the analyst will be forced to aggregate sources into source categories and to study the cost and control options available to each source category. This type of aggregation can lead to situations in which a pollution control source within a certain category has been assumed to adopt a pollution control strategy or technology that, in fact, it would not be capable of using. Therefore, such aggregation assumptions will be open to question by decision makers.

Many other types of aggregation also might be useful in assessing costs and benefits. For example, environmental quality assessments normally will require a certain amount of aggregation over time in order to characterize the environmental quality of the area surrounding a pollution control source. If the regulation is concerned only with annual average air quality, then an annual average of pollutant concentrations might be used in characterizing the environmental quality in the vicinity of, for example, a large-scale power plant. If, on the other hand, a three-hour average is the time dimension used in the proposed regulations, then the aggregation to an annual average will not be acceptable.

Aggregation also may be used when examining the geographic area surrounding the pollution control source. For some pollutants, it may be necessary to develop a physical model of the dispersion of pollution within the immediate vicinity of a pollution source; other pollutants may have only city-wide or county-wide impacts. For example, the geographic area associated with noise pollution is small, while the area associated with the creation of ozone is more extensive.

The pricing behavior of firms within an industry also might have to be aggregated into larger sub-industrial groups in order to perform an Environmental Impact Analysis (EIA) within acceptable budgetary constraints. The willingness to pay of some groups in the community may be different from that of other groups, for example within different income categories. The need to design a strategy to compromise rationally between the degree of detail and the amount of effort expended must be made by the contractor at an early stage of the EIA design.

These aggregation problems can be solved in several ways. An ideal approach would be to aggregate sources, firms, consumer groups, geographic areas, and other factors using one method, do the entire analysis, and then redefine the level of aggregation to determine whether the degree of detail affects the results. This procedure, if feasible, will indicate to the decision makers whether the level of disaggregation chosen was sufficient to ensure that the conclusions of the study would remain valid. It may, however, require a considerable amount of time and effort.

An alternative approach would require the investigator to estimate which areas will come under the greatest amount of controversy or scrutiny during hearings. These areas then would require a larger degree of disaggregation and analysis than would other areas. For example, if the pollution control costs were scrutinized closely by industry but the benefit assessment was not, the investigator may be tempted to disaggregate sources in the part of the study requiring the estimation of costs but not to disaggregate in the environmental quality assessment or in the benefit estimation portion of the study.

A third approach would be to identify that component of the study which, because of the state of the art of analysis, would generate the largest uncertainty with respect to the accuracy of the results. Then, the accuracy of any other component of the study would not be required to be any greater than the component so identified.

The solution to the aggregation design problem will not be amenable to a single guideline that will cover all cases. In part the solution will depend on the nature of the proposal and the objectives of the assessment. If the objective is to minimize error in controversial facets of the proposal, then one design will be used; if the objective is to minimize the maximum degree of error, then another design will be used. If the objective is to assess statistically the error associated with a level of aggregation, then still a different strategy of aggregation and disaggregation will be called for.

Deal Explicitly with Uncertainty, Error, and Bias

All of the sources of uncertainty, error, and bias identified influence the estimates of a proposed regulation's effects and, as noted, will remain at least to some degree in spite of an analyst's best efforts. To summarize, one source of uncertainty is related to assumptions about parameters such as the discount rate. Such parameters are fraught with some degree of uncertainty stemming not from randomness in the data but from difficulties in determining the appropriate conceptual basis for these parameters. Another source of ambiguity is related to uncertainty in prices and costs because of data errors. This would include such examples as randomness in plume models used to translate emissions into ambient air quality, per-unit costs of pieces of equipment, and increases in prices because of increased costs that are likely to be charged. Statistical and other cost-estimation techniques yield further uncertainty.* The technique chosen to estimate costs and benefits should be related to the data and the problem at hand but often the method used depends on the training and bias of the investigator and would not necessarily be related to the regulation itself.

It is difficult to state which factors, and changes in them, are likely to have the greatest influence on the final evaluation. If it were possible to identify the key elements, then an analysis based on the most probable value of these elements, offering also a lower and higher estimate, might be fruitful. It is not clear, however, that this should be done, given the many different uncertainties.

Approaches to handling uncertainty, bias, and error include:

- indicating quantitatively the probability of the estimates' accuracy (in technical parlance, this requires estimating confidence intervals with quantified probability statements);

- presenting high, low, and medium scenarios focusing on the principal policy issues, such as the excess of benefits over costs;

- testing the sensitivity of results to specified data and procedures about which there is no uncertainty;

- communicating sufficiently about the data and procedures to facilitate a subjective judgment by the decision maker about the effects of various sources of uncertainty.

The problems of estimation—including a large number of variables entering into the results and the use of judgment rather than formal statistical techniques at many points—are likely to be far

---

* For example, if instead of using least squares regression, the analyst decided to use some nonparametric technique to form a relationship between the variables, the results might differ. And if an analyst used the factor method of estimating costs coupled with a power rule, the result might be different than if the analyst lumped everything together into a total installed cost for a plant and then used a power rule extrapolation.

too complex to permit formal estimation of confidence intervals. Using judgment to approximate the logic of confidence intervals may nevertheless be useful. Attention must be paid in such an exercise to compound probabilities and to comparable treatment of component variables.

High, medium, and low scenarios can indicate the overall effects of variability, although they lack rigor in the setting of values for various component variables and usually cannot be interpreted statistically. For relatively simple evaluations in which judgment rather than formal statistical estimation is predominant, this type of scenario analysis may be useful. Its usefulness is limited, however, by the fact that the scenario results alone cannot indicate to the decision maker how the various sources of uncertainty contribute to the range of estimates.

Of all the ways of handling uncertainty, error, and bias, sensitivity tests to specified changes in data and procedures have the most to recommend them. The decision maker can relate the cause of change in the estimate to the reason for the change (altered data and procedures) and can judge the likelihood of the change occurring. Some sensitivity tests can be reported in fair detail in the text of a report to a decision maker. Another useful procedure is to report briefly on the outcome of a number of sensitivity tests, so that the decision maker will know that these tests are carried out and will know the sensitivity of results without being overwhelmed by a barrage of numbers pertaining to sensitivity. Test data should be included as an appendix.

Even with very thorough sensitivity tests, there are usually more variables than can be tested. The factors affecting the reliability of estimates should be highlighted in such a way that the decision maker can understand the ranges involved without the benefit of actual numerical comparisons.

CONCLUSION

We have emphasized that benefit-cost analysis is simply an approach to comparing the results of environmental regulation in terms of the values of all the individuals who are affected by it. Costs are a measure of what must be given up to implement regulation; benefits are the effects received in exchange. Since benefits and costs are incommensurate in physical terms, benefit-cost analysts seek to make the comparison easier by expressing the effects in commensurate terms. Expressing effects in dollar terms whenever possible facilitates estimates of the trade-off between benefits or costs and other goods and services that are desired—trade-offs that are inevitable.

The tools of benefit-cost analysis have been drawn from economic analysis over the past 45 years or so and have been applied and refined in hundreds, if not thousands, of studies. While some of the procedures are technical, they are all aimed at discovering as accurately as possible the weights that people attach to what they receive versus what they give up. Benefit-cost analysts make the same kinds of comparisons people make in their everyday life. The past contribution of benefit-cost analysis—and more than ever its usefulness in the future—is based upon the assistance it gives in organizing individual valuations into a coherent and comprehensible way of thinking about environmental actions.*

---

* For additional information on the issues discussed in this essay, refer to:
- Babcock, Croke, Hurter, Loquercio, Roberts, Sievering, and Tolley, *A Handbook for the Assessment of Environmental Benefits and Pollution Control Costs* (Illinois Institute of Natural Resources Document 78/29).
- R. de Neufville and J. Stafford, *Systems Analysis for Engineers and Managers* (McGraw-Hill, 1971).
- H. Peskin and E. Seskin, eds., *Cost/Benefit Analysis and Water Pollution* (Urban Institute, 1975).

6/POLITICS

Cost-Benefit Analysis as Regulatory Reform

Richard N.L. Andrews

Cost-benefit analysis currently is being urged as one of a number of means to reform the regulatory practices of U.S. federal agencies, particularly of those agencies that regulate to protect health, safety, and environmental quality. Murry Weidenbaum, for instance, Chairman of President Reagan's Council of Economic Advisors, recently has called for broader use of cost-benefit analysis in government regulatory proposals, legislatively mandated "economic impact statements," and the modification or elimination of regulations whose costs are judged to be in excess of their benefits.[1] President Reagan himself in February 1981 issued orders requiring that: (1) every executive branch agency prepare a "regulatory impact analysis" identifying the potential costs and benefits of any proposed rule that could lead to "major increases" in consumer prices or industry costs, and describing lower cost alternatives; (2) all major new rules already proposed be postponed until such analyses are completed, unless a statutory or court-imposed deadline or emergency exists; (3) every executive branch agency identify for review and possible change or rescission any existing rules that do not follow the least costly approach; and (4) the Office of Management and Budget (OMB) be authorized to designate regulations as "major" if the agencies do not and to require the agencies to consider additional evidence and information in making their decisions.[2]

* I am grateful to J. Clarence Davies, Maynard M. Hufschmidt, Richard Liroff, Arthur Oleinick, Zygmunt Plater, Gunter Schramm, and Jean Shorett for their most helpful comments on a draft of this paper; to Robert Smythe for several ideas on the NEPA analogy; and to The Conservation Foundation for the opportunity to participate in the conference which was the paper's genesis.

It is not yet clear how much the broader use of such analysis will contribute to meeting the objectives of its advocates, or what it might contribute to or detract from fulfilling the purposes of the regulations. This paper explores the implications of cost-benefit analysis as an instrument of regulatory reform and suggests what appear to be some of its principal strengths and limitations for that purpose. It seems most likely that while the broader required use of cost-benefit analysis may ameliorate some of the problems that concern some regulatory reformers, it will not solve others that are arguably more fundamental; and, depending on how it is mandated and used, it could exacerbate them.

DEFINITION OF COST-BENEFIT ANALYSIS

An unfortunate but pervasive source of frustration in the present debate is a basic lack of consensus on what is meant by cost-benefit analysis. *Formal cost-benefit analysis* is in principle a rigorous, quantitative, and data-intensive procedure, which requires *identification* of all nontrivial effects, *categorization* of these effects as benefits or costs, *quantitative estimation* of the extent of each benefit or cost associated with an action, translation of these into a *common metric* such as dollars, *discounting* of future costs and benefits into the terms of a given year, and *summary* of all the costs and all the benefits to see which is greater.[3] The logic of cost-benefit analysis also demands that these sums be *compared across alternatives*, a point neglected even by many of its proponents.

This definition of cost-benefit analysis traditionally has been used in the analysis of federal water resource projects; since 1973, however, even in this arena cost-benefit analysis has been expanded into a system of multiple objectives and multiple accounts, requiring formal cost-benefit analysis of the costs and benefits to national economic efficiency but separate—and not necessarily commensurable—accounting of desirable and undesirable effects on environmental quality, regional economic development, and "other effects."[4]

The term cost-benefit analysis also recently has been used as a much looser label for several different conceptual frameworks, such as cost-effectiveness analysis, economic impact assessment, and what have been called "regulatory budgets" and "informal cost-benefit analysis."[5]

Cost-effectiveness analysis differs from formal cost-benefit analysis in that it is strictly a comparison among means to a given end. It is used to determine, for example, given a goal of achieving X amount of reduction in air pollution, how much reduction is expected for Y costs associated with a particular action (e.g., a regulation) and whether this is more or less than the cost of an alternative action (or, is there an alternative that could achieve greater reduction for the same or less cost). Unlike formal cost-benefit analysis, it does not attempt to weigh the merits of the goal itself. It does, however, even more clearly require that alternative actions be compared, not simply the costs and effects of a single action.

Economic impact assessment is both simpler and broader than either cost-benefit analysis or cost-effectiveness analysis. It is simpler in that it does not necessarily require aggregation or even categorization of effects as "costs" or "benefits": it requires only the projection of economic effects of proposed actions and the listing of these for consideration. It is broader, however, in that it includes identification of all economic impacts, not simply benefits and costs to economic efficiency. It includes, for instance, changes in the distribution of benefits and costs that might be cancelled out or simply ignored in efficiency analysis. In a sense it is the proper prologue to cost-effectiveness analysis or to formal cost-benefit analysis, but its emphasis is directed toward completeness in the identification of impacts rather than toward a narrower and more selective evaluation of contributions to efficiency. Its output is simply a profile or array of effects rather than cardinal or ordinal decision criteria such as net benefits or cost-effectiveness.

"Regulatory budgets" have been proposed as a means of constraining the aggregate effects of government regulatory requirements on economic activity in a given year. These budgets would set a maximum permissible economic effect level for each agency and require each agency to set priorities accordingly. The concept has been proposed and advocated by various economists and a few legislators but has not yet been described with sufficient specificity to permit detailed discussion.

"Informal cost-benefit analysis" embraces an indefinite range of procedures for generalized identification and balancing of desirable and undesirable effects of proposed actions on society. In its most general form, it approximates pure common sense; almost by definition a government decision reflects the responsible official's judgment that the benefits to society of a particular policy exceed its costs. The questions next arise, however, whether there are particular criteria by which such judgments should be reached and whether such officials should be held more explicitly accountable for their judgments through required documentation of their use of such criteria. Various economists, one U.S. Supreme Court Justice, and at least one plaintiff before the Supreme Court are urging that environmental regulatory agencies—such as the Environmental Protection Agency (EPA) and the Occupational Safety and Health Administration (OSHA)—should be allowed to promulgate rules only if the benefits can be demonstrated to be "reasonably commensurate" with the costs.[6] The key issues in this proposal revolve around the methodological and institutional implications of such a documentation process and the implied substitution of economic efficiency for normative constraints as a basis for decision. These issues will be discussed further below.

The definitional confusion over cost-benefit analysis is not a problem that can be "solved," since like any other label that has taken on political value as a symbol, it inevitably will be used by advocates to "mean what they choose it to mean." It is essential that the problem be recognized, however, as a reminder of the need to probe more specifically the implications of particular proposals to which the label is attached. The protracted political controversies over water resource projects, for instance, have greatly sensitized many advocates of environmental protection to the limitations and abuses of formal cost-benefit analysis in practice, but not all the same objections necessarily apply to cost-effectiveness analysis or more informal cost-benefit analysis.

Beyond misunderstandings over definitions, several levels of issues and disagreements divide proponents and skeptics of the broader use of cost-benefit analysis for regulatory reform. The most fundamental of these involve disagreements over basic philosophies of government; others involve the proper treatment of uncertain and potentially catastrophic hazards, the problems of administrative accountability, and the differences between cost-benefit analysis in principle and in observed practice.

TWO PHILOSOPHIES OF GOVERNMENT

A basic issue in the present debate is the conflict between two sometimes complementary, sometimes opposing philosophies of proper governmental behavior. For this discussion, I shall refer to the first of these as economic optimization and the second as normative constraints.

Economic Optimization

Cost-benefit analysis is grounded in the language, logic, and values of public investment economics. This theoretical framework recognizes three primary justifications for governmental intervention in a market economy: (1) to achieve equity in the distribution of income; (2) to stabilize fluctuations in aggregate economic activity; and (3) to improve economic efficiency—for instance, by correcting market failure (e.g., regulating natural monopolies), providing goods for which markets cannot function ("public goods"), and correcting uncompensated losses and windfall gains to third parties ("externalities").[7] Cost-benefit analysis, as it has been practiced in the past and is still generally practiced today, has concentrated primarily on economic efficiency goals.[8] The fundamental concern underlying this approach is scarcity of resources. Both in government and society, there are never enough resources to do everything that people would like to have done, so choices must be made. The good society is one in which all resources are used for their highest valued purposes, and each of these purposes is achieved in the most efficient and effective way so that no resources are wasted. Good government decisions are those that contribute to achieving these highest valued purposes in the most efficient and effective ways.

Many classes of government action, including some health, safety, and environmental regulations, fall to one degree or another within the philosophical framework of economic optimization. Some actions, such as water resource development projects, traditionally have been subjected to formal cost-benefit analysis to demonstrate that, whatever their other effects, their economic efficiency benefits to society exceed their economic efficiency costs. Other actions, such as many military weapons investments, are expected at least in principle to be cost-effective, though this may or may not be well monitored and enforced in practice. Still others are expected to be "cost sensitive," based on a generalized consideration and balancing of economic implications against other goals on the part of the responsible administrator in the process of pursuing agency missions.[9]

From this philosophy there results a decision framework that is in principle: (1) utilitarian, seeking the "greatest good for the greatest number;" (2) materialistic, measuring the greatest good as much as possible in terms of resources that can be priced; (3) relativistic, willing to constantly trade off increments of any good for any other good in the pursuit of a theoretically efficient optimum, at which no additional change could increase efficiency further; and (4) rationalistic, in its assumption that the relevant facts can be known, weighed, and chosen by experts in the presumed interest of society as a whole.

Normative Constraints

In contrast, other U.S. policies for health, safety, and environmental protection are grounded in an alternative philosophy, the philosophy of normative constraints. As a recent congressional committee report points out, President Lincoln did not sign the Emancipation Proclamation on the basis of its economic efficiency and could not have justified it on that basis had he wished to, nor does society condone murder, theft, perjury, or many other forms of behavior even if their overall economic benefits exceed their costs.[10] These forms of behavior are simply prohibited as unacceptable. Similarly, U.S. health legislation often has been based on the philosophy of protecting citizens as fully as possible from involuntary health hazards, within the constraints of what is technically feasible.

In this conceptual framework, government is not simply a corrective instrument at the margins of economic markets but an equally central arena in which the members of society choose and legitimize—however imperfectly in practice—their collective values. The principal purposes of legislative action are to weigh and affirm social values and to define and enforce the rights and duties of members of the society, through representative democracy. The purpose of administrative action is to put into effect these affirmations by the legislature, not to rebalance them by the criteria of economic theory. Such actions may or may not be directed towards economic efficiency. Economic efficiency is one possible social value that could be chosen, but the lawmaking body may, with equal legitimacy, place a higher value on health, safety, environmental quality, or other purposes such as national defense. In such cases, Congress in effect directs that certain norms be enforced and certain actions required or prohibited, regardless of costs. Equity is assumed to be achieved through the rules of access and other protections that are deliberately built into the Constitution to balance majority and minority interests. Like economic optimization, this philosophy is in principle utilitarian; however, its content is not necessarily materialistic, its choices may set absolute norms or standards as constraints on unacceptable behavior, and its decision method relies on constitutional concepts and procedures—representative government, due process, and equal protection, for instance—rather than economic theory and expert balancing, as a source of decision criteria.

An example suggests additional practical reasons why this second philosophy has come to have such dominant influence in federal environmental protection policy. Prior to 1970, the U.S. Department of Health, Education, and Welfare had authority to set air pollution emissions standards for new motor vehicles, giving "appropriate consideration to technological feasibility and economic costs." This language would clearly permit the use of an economic optimization approach to administrative regulation, although it did not provide authority to change economic incentives (e.g., emissions taxes) as an instrument of that implementation. By 1970, however, it was recognized by Senator Muskie and others that the existing legislation was ineffective, in part because the automobile manufacturers themselves controlled all the relevant data and initiative concerning technological development, thus feasibility and cost, and that, in the six years since the auto manufacturers' 1964 testimony that they were developing alternative technologies, they had made essentially no significant efforts to do so, in Senator Muskie's view.

In the 1970 Clean Air Act amendments, therefore—one of the first major regulatory precedents for the 1970s—Senator Muskie shifted the basis of regulation from feasibility and cost to health criteria, backed by the weight of Congress, as a means of compelling technological change in the unresponsive auto industry. Further, since health effects were not yet well known and standards are easier to relax than to tighten, the standards included a deliberate and substantial margin of safety beyond what could be proven at the time. The result included strict health-based standards (90 percent reduction from 1970-71 levels), strict deadlines for compliance (1975-76), stiff fines for violators, and the removal of discretion from the Executive Branch to postpone compliance. As Senator Muskie put it:

> From a scientific standpoint, you know, [the relation between these emissions criteria and public health] is an uncertain question. . . . But nevertheless, it is a way of establishing a watershed—that is permissible, that side isn't. . . . The health handle . . . is what finally made the Clean Air Act of 1970 possible.[11]

Economic optimization is a powerful ideal and an elegant theory, and Mr. Muskie and others may well have overlooked yet other alternatives; but in the real world of 1970, economic balancing of costs and feasibility against benefits simply was not an effective instrument against the institutional inertia of a major industry. The "health handle," a fixed statutory requirement regardless of costs, was the alternative Congress had available, and it was adopted deliberately as a means of spurring technological innovation that the previous approach did not provide.

A principal consequence of this philosophy is that many laws since have been written as absolute statements defining (and redefining) legal boundaries between particular right and wrong behavior, to be implemented by standards and regulatory commands, rather than as incremental adjustments in economic incentives. According to a report by the U.S. General Accounting Office:

> The Congress adopted regulatory strategies basically centered around the standard setting—monitoring—enforcement regulatory process coupled with uniform effluent and emissions limitation requirements. . . . For various reasons, the Federal strategy is to establish uniform pollution control requirements based on control technology. This strategy is occasionally economically inefficient and in some cases environmentally counterproductive. Why then have environmental programs predominantly resorted to the strict regulatory approach? One reason is that fees entail some uncertainty about the level of cleanup that will be achieved. . . . Large firms with significant market power may prefer merely to pay the fee, rather than make the effort to reduce pollution. . . . In contrast, regulation appears to promise greater certainty on the level of quality to be achieved [although] fee schemes . . . may make adminstration and enforcement more effective and less costly.[12]

SIGNIFICANCE OF PHILOSOPHICAL CONFLICT

The significance of this philosophical conflict can be illustrated in a series of more tangible questions, all of which are at issue in the current debate over use of cost-benefit analysis as regulatory reform.

Should government regulations protect the most sensitive and most heavily exposed members of society, or merely the majority? At one level, this question asks whether society should have regulations pertaining to occupational health, or child labor, or many sorts of pollution at all, since most such hazards affect some groups in society far more intensely than the population as a whole. If one assumes some protection of groups at risk, then one must decide which groups, how many people are in the groups at risk, and from what hazards? Should government regulate the safety of airplane passengers? If so, how about cotton workers and auto passengers? Should air quality standards be set to protect persons afflicted with asthma or emphysema, or just healthy people? Should exposure standards for food additives be strict enough to protect pregnant women and infants, or just nonpregnant adults? Should cotton workers be expected to suffer byssinosis ("brown lung" disease, a painful and often incurable respiratory condition) as a voluntary risk of employment, or invited to wear respirators, or should the cotton industry be expected to install the most effective technology available—engineered ventilation systems—even if costly, so long as it would not force the entire industry out of business? And would the same answer apply if the only cotton workers seriously affected were smokers?[13]

The point here is not simply what the answers to such questions should be but how the answers should be reached. All these answers require public value judgments balancing society's concern and respect for its vulnerable individuals against the general comfort and wealth of the majority. Many such judgments are already expressed in law: both occupational and environmental protection laws balance risk reduction against "feasibility," implying that health is not important enough to justify closure of an entire industry. Advocates of expanded use of cost-benefit analysis urge further steps, balancing the actual cost of that technological change against some quantitative estimate of the resulting benefits. As one economist said in recent testimony:

> If you believe that [technological feasibility] is the proper criteria that OSHA should use, then I think that OSHA has been doing a good job. If that is not the proper criteria, if you think that there ought to be some other notion of weighing the benefits against the costs, then OSHA has not been doing a good job.[14]

The key issue is which of these judgments should be approached through cost-benefit analysis—essentially through a primary concern with economic efficiency—and which should be left to direct moral choice by the legislature, as normative constraints on acceptable behavior. Some proponents of expanded use of cost-benefit analysis, for instance, have advocated it out of anger at decisions that "benefit a narrow constituency at a substantial cost to the rest of society."[15] To others, such protection is simply a legitimate right of persons who are most sensitive or most highly exposed to the hazards of an industrial society. Traditional cost-benefit analysis would not even address this issue as stated, since its concern is solely that the benefits, to whomsoever they may accrue, exceed the costs.

Persons arguing these positions are disagreeing, not just over a method of analysis, but over which social conditions should be treated as moral rights and which should be treated as more variable goals to be weighed against other goals. The willingness even to apply cost-benefit analysis to a particular decision implies an answer to this question.

Which value judgments should be made by the Congress and which by the agency? The normative constraints philosophy implies a dominant role for the legislature, with the regulatory agency as its agent. In principle, the legislature presets certain fundamental value judgments and establishes regulatory authority, goals, and constraints by statute, and the agency then implements these by applying them to the technical subject matter of particular causes and effects. For instance, the legislature requires that the "best practicable technology" be installed to reduce water pollution discharges by a particular date and the agency defines what that technology is for each type of pollution source and then issues and enforces regulations to that effect.

In practice, the agency inevitably make significant value judgments: what practicability really means, in terms of both technological performance and the changes it demands in each industry; how safe is safe enough, for instance in health exposures, given the uncertainties about many dose-response relationships; and, even less often discussed, which hazards to address first and which to let go until later. Most of these judgments, however, still are primarily influenced by the political forces surrounding the agency's relationship to the legislature.

The economic optimization philosophy, in contrast, implies a more autonomous and managerial role for the agency, either on its own or at the direction of the President and Executive Office agencies. To implement this philosophy, the agency must in principle have both the discretionary authority and the responsibility to make value judgments balancing conflicting goals, using regulatory or nonregulatory means, to achieve an economically efficient outcome. For instance, it would need to have authority to decide what types and sources of pollution cause the greatest economic inefficiency and how much pollution was economically efficient to allow, not simply how much would achieve a standard established by law. It also would need authority to seek reduction of increases to that economically efficient level through alternative means such as fees or taxes and regulatory prohibition or mandatory technology.

In practice, agencies normally are not given such broad discretion regarding either means or ends. Moreover, what pressure they experience from the Executive Office is often shaped by judgments no more economically efficient than those of the legislature, reflecting Presidential and OMB political preferences rather than those of the legislature.[16] What discretion they do have is inevitably far more influenced by political opportunities and constraints than by a philosophy of economic optimization. Recently, constituencies who favor economic optimization—allied with others who believe their interest will be served by imposing economic optimization requirements on environmental regulatory agencies—suddenly have greatly increased influence, and the agencies must now respond to a changed political environment.

The point of this question is that the current debate over cost-benefit analysis is, again, not just a technical debate over methodology, but also in part a surrogate for three larger and perennial conflicts: one defining the balance between legislative control and administrative discretion, the second defining the balance between legislative and presidential power, and the third defining ideological preferences favoring or opposing any expansion of government regulatory authority. In principle cost-benefit analysis is a neutral methodology, at least if one accepts the primacy of economic efficiency as a social goal (or even the relevance of examining the effects of proposed actions on economic efficiency, whether or not it is considered primary.) In practice, its use increases the agency's accountability to those whose benefits and costs are most concentrated and most readily measurable and to the OMB but it simultaneously, and significantly, decreases the agency's accountability to the legislature and to the other groups most affected by the problems the agency was established to address. These groups include, of course, both victims of the problem and those who make their livings solving it by the particular standards and in the particular ways specified by the legislature.

Should government permit or prohibit hazards whose dangers, and/or the effectiveness of whose reduction, are not well understood? Like the previous two questions, this raises an issue far broader than the use of cost-benefit analysis, but one which is directly involved in the current debate and in the philosophical conflict between economic optimization and normative constraints. Cost-benefit analysis emphasizes choosing rationally on the basis of what is knowable. This is in fact the principal argument for it, that it forces systematic thought and explicit reasoning by public officials who may otherwise be biased, overzealous, irresponsible, or simply thoughtless of the consequences of their actions. The same logic favors the use of cost-benefit analysis for decisions in which the most important benefits and costs are reasonably knowable. For the same reason, however, cost-benefit analysis may be of more debatable or even negative value for hazards whose dangers are of great concern but very uncertain, for it tends toward a policy that may underestimate the value of judgment and the cost of dread. This point is well illustrated, perhaps unintentionally, by the recent testimony of one leading proponent of cost-benefit analysis:

> It makes it more difficult to assert a purported health or safety benefit for which there is no evidence. In short, the excuse for avoiding cost-benefit analysis is likely to be one which argues strongly against regulation at all— or at least against using any decision making tool other than the rolling of dice.[17]

At face value such a statement is quite compelling. It passes over, however, a more difficult issue: how should government treat hazards in which catastrophic potential is combined with great uncertainty? If the uncertainty concerns the causal significance of a particular activity, should the government prohibit this activity until it is proven acceptably safe—as is now done for new drugs—or should it permit the activity until it is proven hazardous, as is now done for pesticides and many other chemicals?

If the uncertainty concerns the effectiveness of a regulatory remedy, should the remedy be postponed until its effectiveness can be documented or should the remedy be invoked, if it reflects the best judgment of those familiar with the problem, and its effectiveness monitored? The answers to these questions imply opposite burdens of risk—victims versus those who cause hazards—and opposite burdens of proof—agencies versus those who cause hazards.

There is no disagreement that the best evidence should be gathered to understand hazards and to improve the effectiveness of their remedies. There is, however, disagreement as to whether government should be risk-tolerant or risk-averse towards uncertain but potentially catastrophic hazards, as to who should bear the risks and who the burden of proof, and as to whether or not cost-benefit analysis in current practice is neutral toward these questions. The more quantitatively cost-benefit analysis is used, the more it may be expected to emphasize the knowable over the uncertain, the identifiable over the widely dispersed, the calculable over the difficult to calculate, the present over the future. In situations of uncertainty and catastrophic potential, the reduction of all potential sources of threat may well be a justifiable alternative philosophy, at least as an initial policy to be followed by monitoring for effectiveness and other consequences.

Which hazards need or deserve treatment by normative constraints? The questions above raise important issues of principle, but they do not necessarily imply that every hazard deserves to be addressed by normative constraints rather than economic optimization. Indeed, many already are treated by economic principles. It is appropriate to consider, therefore, whether there may be hazards which either should first be addressed in the framework of economic optimization or which should be shifted—based on, for instance, experience with their regulations or new information about their causes and significance—from one approach to the other. In some cases, as with the Clean Air Act of 1970, it may be necessary to make constraints stronger than those brought about by the usual practice of economic balancing. In others, normative constraints may be ineffective or unnecessary, and a switch to economic balancing may thus be appropriate.

PRINCIPLE VERSUS PRACTICE

The questions raised above illustrate some of the more fundamental and difficult issues that are implicated in the debate over whether, and to what extent, cost-benefit analysis is appropriate as an instrument for analyzing regulatory proposals. A second and pragmatic level of issues arises from the history of cost-benefit analysis in practice. Like any procedure, its actual application does not necessarily fulfill its theoretical potential: in part because of insufficient effort and expertise; in part because rigorous cost-benefit analysis is not always itself a cost-effective use of scarce resources.

The history of cost-benefit analysis is a history of two intertwined threads. One thread is the history of the idealism of many people, economists and others, who aspire to a society based on science and research—a society which more explicitly analyzes its decisions and weeds out ignorance and irrationality. Many such people also believe, with genuine idealism, that making society more efficient will expand the available resources for everyone and thus mitigate, if not solve, more difficult issues such as distributional equity. Some might add that when many important decisions must, because of their technicality, be shaped by experts in government bureaucracies, cost-benefit analysis also provides a valuable tool of accountability which is thereby supportive of democratic ideals against arbitrary authority.

The second thread is the history of the persistent use of analytical requirements such as cost-benefit analysis to support particular political purposes and constituencies. Applied to water resource projects, for instance, cost-benefit analysis has been a fertile field for the development of economic theory and public investment principles. It was also quite clearly fostered and constrained by the Bureau of the Budget, using a narrower range of measures than could have been justified as a political weapon against the "pork barrel" process by which Congress authorizes water projects.[19] The Planning-Programming-Budgeting System (PPBS), Management by Objectives (MBO), and Zero-Base Budgeting (ZBB), all advocated in principle as methods for more informed analysis of government programs and expenditure proposals, in practice were mandated from the top as instruments for increasing executive control over administrative agencies.[20] Environmental impact assessment, which like cost-benefit analysis ideally is a way of making decision consequences more explicit, serves also as a political tactic for delaying or stalemating projects that some interest groups do not want.[21]

The current pressure for use of cost-benefit analysis for environmental regulations incorporates both these threads. It is in part a sincere effort by some economists and others to improve governmental decision making, to make trade-offs explicit, and to point out the illogic and high cost of some decisions that are being made. But it is equally, on the part of other constituencies, a political weapon for challenging the recent primacy of environmental, health, and safety concerns and other consumer values, and for attempting to substitute for these a greater emphasis on business and producer values. In practice cost-benefit analysis relies heavily on estimates that can only be provided by the business regulated, estimates that sometimes have been inflated;[22] it grew from heavy business lobbying and advertising compaigns attacking the alleged cost of environmental regulations;[23] it is being used by business interest groups as a weapon of delay or stalemate against government regulations that raise the cost of doing business.[24] Cost-benefit analysis also has been used as a weapon by Executive Office agencies, using assumptions no less arbitrary or subjective than those of the regulatory agencies, to seek substantive change in the agencies' priorities.[25]

Much of the current resistance to cost-benefit analysis of environmental regulations comes, not from people who are ignorant of its merits in principle, nor from people who are narrowly self-interested, but from people who believe—correctly or not—that business economics already has a pervasive influence on public debate, that its quantifiable dollar metric already exerts a disproportionately coercive force on the shape of public policy, and that the translation of debates over environment, health, and safety into the terms of investment economics will increase this dominance. To them the question is not how cost-benefit analysis could be used, but how it is being used and likely will be used, and whether or not that usage provides an appropriate primary framework for public policy decisions. Thus far, in the new proposals for cost-benefit analysis, there appears to be little evidence of the development of safeguards against repetition of past abuses.

THE NEPA ANALOGY

The National Environmental Policy Act (NEPA) provides what may be an exceptionally apt analogy for predicting the effects of using cost-benefit analysis as an instrument of regulatory reform. NEPA is best known for its requirements that a "detailed statement" be prepared for every "major federal action significantly affecting the quality of the human environment;" that this statement discuss the action's impacts, adverse effects, alternatives, and other matters; and that the statement be circulated for review and comment to all other affected agencies and made available to the public along with those agencies' comments before the action is taken.[26] This charge applies to all agencies of the federal government and has led to the preparation of some 1,000 to 1,400 of these "environmental impact statements" (EISs) per year since 1970, including many on government regulatory actions (though certain large classes of environmental regulatory actions by EPA are exempted by statute).

The EIS is but one of a set of mutually reinforcing mandates established by NEPA. The law's core is a statement of policy goals expressing Congress' intent that the actions of the federal government

be directed toward harmonizing relationships between human activities and the natural processes upon which they depend. The EIS
is one of a series of so-called "action forcing" provisions, procedural requirements explicitly intended to insure that all agencies
consider the policy mandate in their daily activities and routines.
Other procedural mandates required that agencies develop
methods and procedures "to insure appropriate consideration of
presently unquantified environmental amenities and values." Finally, NEPA established an institutional focal point for oversight of
the law's implementation, the Council on Environmental Quality,
(CEQ) to advise the President and to guide agencies on an ongoing
basis.[27]

Substantive Intent

NEPA obviously differs profoundly from current cost-benefit analysis proposals in its substantive intent. One of the chief reasons for
its enactment, in fact, was the disenchantment of its proponents
with existing requirements that agencies choose least-cost or greatest net-benefit solutions—for instance, for highway routes and water resource projects—regardless of other values, harder to monetize, that thereby were lost. By judicial interpretation, NEPA was
held to require "balancing" of economic and environmental benefits and costs, as advocates of cost-benefit analysis today point out,
but the point of these decisions was that *environmental* considerations must be added to balances which already tended to over-
weigh *economic* considerations rather than vice versa.[29] And NEPA
explicitly did not require that intangible values be quantified—only
that they be given "appropriate consideration" by the agency's procedures.[30]

Procedural Means

Despite the difference of substantive intent, NEPA and today's
cost-benefit analysis proposals are strikingly similar in their procedural purposes and method. Like NEPA, the Reagan administration's cost-benefit analysis mandate expresses a substantive
philosophy—that government regulations should in effect be as
harmonious as possible with the American business environment
and should choose the alternative that is least costly in its impact on
that environment. The administration is implementing that mandate both by "action-forcing" documentation requirements and by

authorizing an institutional monitor in the Executive Office—the OMB—to oversee and influence the agencies' implementation of the policy mandate.[31]

Both NEPA and cost-benefit analysis in short, are intended as instruments of administrative reform, and while the substantive intentions of their advocates differ, they use strikingly similar means in the pursuit of those ends.[32] Like cost-benefit analysis, NEPA was deliberately used by its sponsors as a means of achieving sweeping substantive changes through procedural means—of requiring in all agencies a different balance among decision considerations than could have been achieved by amending each agency's authorizing statutes one at a time.[33]

Manipulable Analyses

Two additional similarities are also evident. First, both environmental impact assessment and cost-benefit analysis are, in general use, highly inexact and manipulable methods of analysis. At best, each is capable of great comprehensiveness and precision, but neither the resources nor the requisite time of trained professionals—nor in some cases, the requisite professional consensus on methods and assumptions—exist to insure this. As a result, both methods are highly susceptible to charges of arbitrariness, subjectivity, and self-interest in the range of alternatives examined, in the choice of data and impacts of each, and in other highly influential assumptions such as the discount rate, the value of life, and the probability of future events.[34]

Depending on the assumptions used, for instance, environmental impact assessments have been claimed to either support or oppose such major environmental modifications as the Trans-Alaska Pipeline System and the MX Missile System. Similar choices among even more plausible assumptions could easily cause cost-benefit analysis to appear to support opposite decisions involving many environmental regulations.

In short, cost-benefit analysis will not provide an unambiguous method of reaching decisions about most proposed regulations; it will provide at best only one array of relevant information bearing on such decisions. Under such circumstances, the formal content of the analysis may be expected to be much less an influence in its own right than a by-product of the political and institutional dynamics shaping the analytical process.

Paperwork and Coordination

A second similarity between NEPA and current cost-benefit analysis proposals is that both rely on broad new paperwork requirements and review processes as their principal tools, rather than on direct substantive changes in the agencies' statutory missions and priorities. The official rationale for such tools is that they insure comprehensive thought: by forcing the administrator to consider all significant consequences, it is assumed they lead to better reasoned decisions. There has been vigorous discussion of the merits of such tools in the case of NEPA, in which opponents have argued strenuously that administrators neither can nor should think comprehensively, that such comprehensive rationality is not even a good ideal for administrative decision making, and that such tools are therefore a wasteful diversion of resources.[35] Precisely the same arguments can be made for or against any general requirement for cost-benefit analysis documentation.

Both sides of this argument, however, miss the more significant—and perhaps, more deliberate—practical and political rationale for such tools. The effective rationale is that such tools increase the influence of certain kinds of information in the decision process; that they thus increase the power and access of constituencies who control those kinds of information; and that they tend to cause change, delay, or reversal of proposals that do not bode well—whatever their other merits—in terms of the new information and paperwork requirements. These tools are unquestionably a blunt and inefficient means of change for they increase rather than decrease the administrative costs and delays of taking action, and they work only by the indirection of political negotiations over the analyses rather than by direct clarification of value priorities. But they are, arguably, the most effective means available—despite their administrative inefficiency—for achieving the substantive purposes of their proponents.

Visibility of Analysis

Despite the considerable similarities metioned above, three important differences must be noted between NEPA and current cost-benefit analysis proposals. First, NEPA created an analytical requirement with highly visible outputs, accessible to all persons who might be affected by proposed actions, and open to comment, correction, and judicial review. There is good evidence that this public disclosure process has been the principal source of NEPA's value as an administrative reform and that it has greatly helped to equalize access to the administrative decision process for potential victims as well as for beneficiaries of proposed actions.[36]

Detractors, however, would conclude from the same evidence that it has greatly politicized such processes. Cost-benefit analysis requirements in their present form do not include any such mechanisms for interagency review and public disclosure. The most likely sources of influence on the analyses, therefore, are those who have identifiable economic stakes in the outcomes, such as the OMB and, through it, businesses that would experience the direct costs of proposed regulations (even if these costs were less than more broadly dispersed social benefits).

Asymmetric Application

Second, while NEPA was required for all types of government activities that might have significant environmental effects, current cost-benefit analysis requirements apply only to government regulatory proposals, not to all actions that might inflict significant social costs. It may be argued that regulations are singled out because other actions are subject to such analyses anyway through the annual budgetary process, which regulations had heretofore escaped, but this is not always true. Many government policies are carried out through off-budget mechanisms; major expenditures are made by formula or by normative assumptions, without meaningful comparative analysis of costs, benefits and alternatives. To the extent that cost-benefit analysis is imposed on health, safety, and environmental regulations but not on these other activities— moreover, even to the extent that the paperwork, other transaction costs, and practical politics of cost-benefit analysis documentation are imposed on such regulations but not on other activities—the latter may be expected to absorb excessive resources and to continue to inflict greater social costs than justified.

Least Harmful Alternative

NEPA never explicitly required that agencies choose the alternative least harmful to environmental quality, though one of its apparent assumptions was that if agencies were required to explicitly discuss and consider such an alternative they would more likely be led to choose it by the force of their own logic (or by associated political persuasion). The Reagan administration's cost-benefit analysis mandate, in contrast, does require agencies to choose "the alternative involving the least net cost to society—taking into account the condition of the particular industries affected by regulations [and] the condition of the national economy."[37] If considering "least net cost to society" in a broad sense, it could be argued that such a requirement need not differ greatly in principle from harmony between human activities and environmental conditions, the mandate of NEPA. In the context of the qualifying phrases, however, and in the institutional context of the proposed cost-benefit analysis requirement (asymmetric application, less visible decisions, an avowedly antiregulatory administration, proposed abolition of CEQ, and strengthened oversight authority in OMB) one may reasonably anticipate a much narrower interpretation of what "costs" to society are to be included in the analysis. A predictable result will be that equally real social costs, which are more widely dispersed, more difficult to measure, or incompletely reflected in current measures of the economy (e.g., Gross National Product and the Consumer Price Index), will be ignored; and the indisputable inefficiencies of some present regulations simply wil be replaced, or conceivably even increased, by the inefficiencies of new ones.

EXPECTED RESULTS

From the foregoing analyses, the following can reasonably be expected to be primary effects of current efforts to use cost-benefit analysis as an instrument of regulatory reform.

Stopping the "Worst"

Cost-benefit analysis requirements will almost certainly stop a number of proposals that appear hardest to justify by the conventional methods and assumptions of cost-benefit analysis procedures; they also will undoubtedly stop an undeterminable number of other such proposals from being proposed in the first place. As in the case of NEPA, the number of actions ultimately affected in this way will probably be less than its supporters will wish to claim but also greater than can be proven empirically—even by cost-benefit analysis. Some of these actions will be genuinely worth stopping. Others, however, will be arguably desirable actions in terms of their broad social costs and benefits, but either will not fit the narrower formulas and assumptions by which implementation will actually proceed or will be opposed by OMB or the President for other policy or political reasons. Still others, of a very different sort, may be initiatives desired by the new Administration that are vulnerable to the same challenges from advocates of the status quo; issues on which liberal Democrats can hoist the Administration by its own petard. As at least one conservative commentator has suggested:

> Unless the requirements are carefully drawn so as to apply only to rules that increase the burdens imposed on the private sector, extant regulations will be accorded a sort of presumptive validity, and the elimination of regulations will be subjected to a burden of proof that the original adoption of regulation never confronted. *In some areas, it may be impossible to sustain that burden of proof. . . because of the irremediable absence of data.*[35] [emphasis added: the statement also suggests the political rather than "neutral" intent of at least this advocate of regulatory cost-benefit analysis.]

Cost Sensitive vs. Technological Constraints

It is obvious that the broad requirement of cost-benefit analysis will shift some regulations from a normative constraint to at least a more cost-sensitive basis, if not to formal cost-benefit analysis or cost-effective analysis, especially those whose statutes are subject to some discretion for administrative interpretation on this point. It is not yet clear how many this category will include, nor how many of those should be moved in light of the hazards involved and the availability of other economically demonstrable means of protection against them.

Legitimize the Status Quo

At the agency level, cost-benefit analysis will also, as its advocates desire, almost certainly retard the development of new regulatory initiatives, but it will not by itself reduce the onus of existing ones. At best, it may well stimulate agencies to creativity in developing nonregulatory alternatives. Such creativity will be limited, however, both by existing statutory constraints and by the perception that even the new idea would require revision of existing regulations, which in turn would expose the agency to the unwanted risks of OMB and Administration scrutiny. Cost-benefit analysis will not, in short, stop regulations, as much as it will have a chilling effect on regulations, whether these are considered good or bad. It will thus tend to legitimize most of the status quo, with the exception of a relatively small number of particular targets and particular initiatives—especially those identified for explicit change by the

Regulatory Task Force chaired by the Vice President. Within the agencies it will legitimize the status quo by making regulatory change more difficult. Outside government it will legitimize the status quo by assuming existing economic conditions as a basis for cost-benefit analysis, since cost-benefit analysis may tend to over-estimate compliance costs and to underestimate the savings caused by technological innovations for compliance.

Social vs. Administrative Efficiency

To the extent that cost-benefit analysis is applied properly and successfully, it should increase overall economic efficiency in the society by insuring that the benefits of government regulations, in efficiency terms, exceed their costs. It is not yet clear whether or not that result will be achieved, but it is likely that, as with EISs, administrative inefficiency will be increased in the process: increased paperwork, yet more studies and delays before government can act, negotiation between the agencies and OMB, new rounds of court tests on the guidelines, methods, and assumptions. How great these increases may be, and whether or not they exceed the expected benefits, are not yet clear. Much will depend on how narrow a methodology OMB seeks to impose, how broad a range of agency actions it tries to impose cost-benefit analysis on, and how forcefully it attempts to use cost-benefit analysis to reduce the agencies' power and autonomy.

Centralization of Power

The requirement of cost-benefit analysis will almost certainly increase the power of the President and OMB relative to agencies, the Congress, and the victims and beneficiaries of particular regulations; it will also increase the power of upper level administrators within the agencies over bureaus and other subunits, and the power of staff economists in Washington over line managers in the field. This will occur because cost-benefit analysis is heavily shaped by assumptions controlled by Washington administrators and their staff experts, it requires analyses better understood and more useful to the central executive in Washington than to others, and it increases the opportunity for central administrators to veto lower-level proposals that do not "fit" in that analytical system. The positive view of such an effect is that it makes government more accountable to its management hierarchy and ultimately to the President; the negative view is that it diminishes the values frequently associated with a more decentralized government, such as flexibility to local conditions and responsiveness to the needs and problems of those more directly affected by government actions. In this effect cost-benefit analysis may differ significantly from NEPA, since the public review procedures associated with NEPA served much more to promote pluralism in the decision process than cost-benefit analysis managed by OMB. (Note, however, that environmental regulatory agencies have not always been known for exhibiting great flexibility and responsiveness to local conditions.)

Tool, Not Rule

Like environmental impact assessment, cost-benefit analysis at its best may provide a valuable analytical framework for systematically considering the relative merits of proposed government actions, and for insuring consideration of one array of relevant consequences of such actions. It can in this sense be a valuable tool for analyzing many choices. However, neither now nor perhaps ever can it provide an adequate and unambiguous rule for making most major government decisions. This conclusion is especially true for choices involving the ends (as opposed to the means) of government action. It frequently can, for instance, help to discriminate among more and less costly means of achieving a chosen standard, and it may sometimes assist in setting priorities among regulatory mandates to enforce. It cannot, however, show what the "proper" standards should be in the first place, nor—unless least-cost in a narrow sense is the only decision criterion—can it provide a clear decision among alternative means. This point seems widely accepted among economists but may frustrate the hopes of some less knowledgeable advocates. It is simply, as one economist recently put it in Congressional testimony, too primitive a tool for that sort of use.[39] Knowledge will always be incomplete, and health and safety will always require social value judgments broader than those which cost-benefit analysis or economic efficiency goals can provide.

Statutory Constraints

Many advocates of cost-benefit analysis assume that most regulatory problems arise from heedlessness of costs on the part of bureaucrats. This is undoubtedly true in some cases. In many other cases, however—perhaps even most—the officials' behavior arises not from personal heedlessness but from statutory constraints: statutory goals and principles, statutory criteria and standards, statutory procedures and restrictions on authorized alternatives. For example, EPA has authority to regulate effluent discharges and to finance waste treatment plants, but it does not have authority to levy effluent taxes. OSHA has authority to require feasible technological safeguards against workplace health hazards; it does not, it argues, have authority to balance the cost of preventing those hazards against the economic benefits of workers' health.

The Congress can change such constraints if it chooses to do so. The requirement of cost-benefit analysis by executive order, however, does not change these constraints and therefore should not be expected to bring about many of the changes in regulatory behavior that some of its advocates might wish. It may influence some such constraints by subversion, as NEPA's process may have subverted the existing statutory missions of the public works resource development agencies. There are limits to what should or can be done by such means, however. In particular, subversion can stop some actions not desired but cannot facilitate better alternatives that are not yet authorized by statute.

Program Priorities vs. Individual Actions

There is a natural tendency to focus too narrowly, as with NEPA's EIS requirement, on the immediate effect of cost-benefit analysis requirements on regulatory proposals already "in the pipeline" and on individual regulatory actions generally. I believe this would be a mistake, not only for regulatory reformers but also for the agencies being reformed. Retroactive analysis sets bad precedents; retroactive preparation of EISs has been widely blamed for many of the paperwork excesses, bad and half-hearted analyses, and diversion of effort that compromised NEPA's effectiveness and distorted its intent.[40] More generally, however, the individual regulation simply is not the best target for effective cost-benefit analysis.

The greatest positive potential of cost-benefit analysis lies at a higher level: the level at which programmatic priorities must be set among mandates to be pursued. Most agencies have more to do than their resources permit.[41] EPA and OSHA are no exceptions. To which mandates, therefore should they dedicate their staffs and budgets? Air pollution, water pollution, or toxic chemical dumps? PCBs, lead, oxides of sulfur and nitrogen, or urea formaldehyde? Drinking water or wastewater? Cost-benefit analysis can probably help more positively in these sorts of decisions—in which the agency has great discretion and in which tremendous variance in actual health and environmental protection may hang on the agency's choice—than in simply justifying the individual regulatory actions developed later in the process.

The Reagan Executive Order does direct the agencies to set regulatory priorities, not just to analyze individual regulatory proposals; this, however, will undoubtedly require vigorous emphasis if the tendency to overemphasize justification of individual actions is to be avoided.

Systematic Thinking vs. Systematic Action

Finally, cost-benefit analysis is not a panacea for the problems of proliferation, overlap, and inconsistency among regulatory requirements and agencies—problems that so frustrate the business community. It may increase systematic thinking about individual actions, and perhaps even about individual programs, but it does not address inefficiencies and other problems arising from a lack of coordination among actions or programs. For these problems, other means of regulatory reform will be necessary.

CONCLUSION

It is clear that cost-benefit analysis can contribute usefully to the political process if it is used judiciously, selectively, and in an honest effort to inform choice and to foster logical reasoning and analysis in administrative agencies. It is equally clear that cost-benefit analysis has not always achieved these contributions, that it sometimes has been used for different or opposite purposes, and that current demands for its extension to environmental regulations are being made side by side with inflated claims of the costs of proposed regulations to business. How then, can we best use cost-benefit analysis?

First, it would help to reject three notions: that formal cost-benefit analysis should be conducted for all environmental regulatory decisions, that all decision considerations should be expressed in economic terms, and that cost-benefit analysis provides a rule or overall framework for making such decisions. Economic analysis can illuminate some important consequences of many decisions, and in these circumstances can obviously help to inform the broader political process; but in many cases limited forms of economic analysis, such as economic impact assessment and cost-effectiveness analysis, may prove more useful and acceptable and even more cost-effective than formal cost-benefit analysis.

Second, it would help to put primary emphasis not just on individual regulatory proposals but on the broader processes by which major decisions are framed, evaluated, and chosen. For particular regulations people could build on the process of "scoping" developed for environmental analysis by the CEQ.[42] The key element in this process is a serious and early effort to engage all interested parties in identifying the range of values affected by a decision, the alternatives to be considered, and the analyses needed to frame the choices among them. Economic analysis would likely be one major input in many decisions but not necessarily in all. For setting priorities among hazards, and between regulatory and nonregulatory means of reducing those hazards, cost-benefit analysis has perhaps far greater value as an analytical framework than it will have as mere documentation for justifying particular proposals already developed.

Third, and finally, it would help greatly if those who are most knowledgeable of the economic validity of cost-benefit analysis would be more outspokenly intolerant of those who use it inaccurately or misleadingly—for instance, by treating increased business costs as synonymous with inflation, by exaggerating potential costs of proposed actions, by ignoring some sorts of costs and benefits, and by implying that the economic conclusions embrace all relevant decision considerations.

Cost-benefit analysis is a useful instrument for some kinds of regulatory reform which now seem timely. It is not, however, a panacea for all needs. It is costly to use, costlier to use properly, and it rarely provides unambiguous answers. At its best it may improve some decisions; improperly used, it may do the opposite, and subvert regulatory actions that should be taken to protect public health, safety, and environmental quality, and to remedy other real externalities and hazards. It should not be used as a political weapon beyond its own legitimate purposes, validity, or cost-effectiveness.

Notes

1. Murray L. Weidenbaum, *The Future of Business Regulation* (New York: Amacom, 1980), pp. 62-67, 124-129.

2. Executive Order 12291, Feb. 19, 1981.

3. U.S. Congress, House Committee on Interstate and Foreign Commerce, Subcommittee on Oversight and Investigations and on Consumer Protection and Finance, *Use of Cost-Benefit Analysis by Regulatory Agencies*, Joint Hearings, 96th Congress, 1st Session, July and October 1979, Serial No. 96-157. Testimony of Lester B. Lave, pp. 11-12.

4. U.S. Water Resources Council, "Principles and Standards for Planning Water and Related Land Resources." 38 Fed. Reg. 24778-869 (Sept. 10, 1973); revised 44 Fed. Reg., 72978 (Dec. 14, 1979), and 45 Fed. Reg. 29302 (April 4, 1980).

5. Lave testimony, note 3 above.

6. Lave testimony, ibid. at p. 99; Justice Powell, concurring opinion in *Industrial Union Department, AFL-CIO v. American Petroleum Institute*, 10 ELR 20489, 20504 (U.S., 1980); *American Textile Manufacturers Institute v. Marshall* and *National Cotton Council of America v. Marshall*, U.S. Supreme Court Docket Nos. 79-1429 and 79-1583.

7. Richard A. Musgrave, *The Theory of Public Finance* (New York: McGraw-Hill, 1959), pp. 6-17.

8. Gunter Schramm, "Accounting for Non-economic Goals in Benefit-Cost Analysis," 1 *J. of Envr. Mgt.*, (1973), pp. 129-150.

9. See William H. Rodgers, Jr., "Benefits, Costs and Risks: Oversight of Health and Environmental Decisionmaking." 4 *Harvard Envr. L. Rev.* 191 (1980).

10. U.S. Congress, House Committee on Interstate and Foreign Commerce, Subcommittee on Oversight and Investigations, *Cost-Benefit Analysis: Wonder Tool or Mirage?* 96th Congress, 2nd Session, Committee Print 96-IFC62, pp. 5-6.

11. Reported in Harvard University, John F. Kennedy School of Government, *Senator Muskie and The 1970 Amendments to the Clear Air Act*, Case Study No. C94-76-140, 1976.

12. U.S. General Accounting Office, *Environmental Protection Issues in the 1980s*, Rept. No. CED-81-83 (Dec. 30, 1980), pp. 10-11.

13. Cotton dust cases, cited in note 6 above; also "Perspectives: The Cotton Dust Case," 5 *Regulation* 5-6 (Jan./Feb. 1981).

14. Lave testimony, op. cit. at p. 96.

15. Testimony of Robert W. Crandall, House Hearings (note 3 above) at p. 56.

16. Michael S. Baram, "Cost-Benefit Analysis: An Inadequate Basis for Health, Safety, and Environmental Regulatory Decisionmaking," 8 *Ecol. L.Q.* 473 (1980).

17. Crandall testimony, op. cit.

18. On catastrophic potential see Paul Slovic, Baruch Fischhoff, and Sarah Lichtenstein, "Facts and Fears: Understanding Perceived Risk," in R.C. Schwing and W.A. Albers, Jr. (eds.), *Societal Risk Assessment: How Safe is Safe Enough?* (New York: Plenum 1980) pp. 207-210.

19. Richard N.L. Andrews, *Environmental Policy and Administrative Change* (Lexington, MA: Lexington Books, 1976), pp. 49-51.

20. Aaron Wildavsky, *The Politics of the Budgetary Process* (Boston: Little, Brown, 3rd ed. 1979), chapter 6.

21. E. Bardach and L. Pugliaresi, "The Environmental Impact Statement vs. the Real World," 49 *The Public Interest* 22 (1977); R. Andrews, "NEPA in Practice: Environmental Policy or Administrative Reform?" 6 *Envr. L. Reptr.* 50001-09 (1976).

22. House Committee Report, op. cit. at pp. 11-16 (note 10); Putnam, Hayes, and Bartlett, Inc., "Comparisons of Estimated and Actual Pollution Control Capital Expenditures for Selected Industries" (Contract Study for U.S. EPA, June 1980).

23. House Hearings, op. cit. at p. 312. (note 3).

24. E.g., Ibid., testimony of Murray L. Weidenbaum, pp. 319-24.

25. Baram, op. cit.

26. Public Law 91-190, Sec. 102 (2))C), 42 U.S.C. §4321 *et. seq.*

27. Ibid.

28. Andrews, *Environmental Policy and Administrative Change,* op. cit. Chapter 2.

29. E.g., *Calvert Cliffs Coordinating Committee vs. Atomic Energy Commission,* 449 F. 2nd 1109; See also F.R. Anderson, *NEPA in the Courts* (Baltimore: Johns Hopkins, 1973), pp. 256-58.

30. NEPA Sec. 102 (2) (B); R. Andrews and M. J. Waits, *Environmental Values in Public Decisions* (Ann Arbor: Univ. of Michigan, School of Natural Resources, 1978), chapter 1.

31. Exec. Order 12291, op. cit.

32. Andrews, "NEPA in Practice," op. cit.

33. Andrews, *Environmental Policy and Administrative Change,* op. cit. Chapter 2.

34. Harold Feiveson *et al. Boundaries of Analysis* (Cambridge, MA: Ballinger, 1976); Bruce Bartlett, "Does Econometrics Add Up?" *Policy Review* No. 14 (Fall 1980), pp. 67-82.

35. Andrews, "NEPA in Practice," op. cit.; S. K. Fairfax, "A Disaster in the Environmental Movement," 199 *Science* 743-48 (Feb. 17, 1978).

36. Andrews, ibid.; R. Andrews, "Class Politics or Democratic Reform? Environmentalism and American Political Institutions," 20 *Natural Resources J.* 221-242, (1980).

37. Executive Order 12291, op. cit.

38. Antonin Scalia, "Viewpoint: Regulatory Reform—The Game has Changed," 5 *Regulation* 14 (Jan./Feb. 1981).

39. E.g., House Hearings (note 3 above), Lave testimony at p. 99.

40. R. Andrews, "NEPA in Practice," op. cit., also R. Gillette, "National Environmental Policy Act: How Well is it Working?" 176 *Science* 146-50 (1972); and L. R. Caldwell, "The Environmental Impact Statement: A Misused Tool," in R. K. Jain and B. L. Hutchings (eds.) *Environmental Impact Analysis: Emerging Issues in Planning* (Urbana: U. of Illinois Press, 1978), pp. 11-25.

41. R. Andrews, "Environment and Energy: Implications of Overloaded Agendas," 19 *Nat. Res. J.* 187-504 (1979).

42. U.S. Council on Environmental Quality, "Regulations for Implementing the Procedural Provisions of NEPA," 40 CFR Part 1501.7.

7/ETHICS

Cost-Benefit Analysis and Environmental, Safety, and Health Regulation: Ethical and Philosphical Considerations

Steven Kelman

At the broadest level, cost-benefit analysis may be regarded simply as systematic thinking about decision making. Who can oppose, indignant proponents of cost-benefit analysis frequently ask critics, efforts to think systematically about the various consequences of alternative decisions? The alternative, it would appear, is unexamined or idiosyncratic decision making.

Equating cost-benefit analysis with an attempt to ponder systematically the consequences of decisions deprives the concept of many implications for actual decisions faced by regulatory officials. I will assume therefore, that those who argue that "more cost-benefit analysis is needed" in decisions involving environmental, safety, and health regulation hold views such as the following:

- An act should not be undertaken unless its benefits outweigh its costs. (More formally, economists would argue that the right decision is one in which the excess of benefits over costs is maximized. Thus, a decision with benefits of 100x and costs of 99x would be wrong if there were an alternative decision with benefits of 100x and costs of 95x.)

- To determine whether benefits outweigh costs, all benefits and costs should be expressed in a common metric, so that they can be compared with one another, since some benefits and costs are not traded on markets and hence have no established dollar values.

- Efforts to increase both the degree to which decision makers account for costs and benefits and the accuracy of calculating costs and benefits are important enough to warrant the use of persuasion and politics (as well as the expenditure of money) to give these efforts greater public priority than other types of decision analysis.

I wish to examine each of these three views from a perspective of philosophical discourse, and more particularly from the perspective of formal ethical theory; that is, the study of what actions are morally right (or wrong) to undertake. About the first of the presumptions—the view that an act is right if its benefits outweigh its costs and wrong if its benefits do not—there is an enormous amount of discussion in ethical theory; indeed, it is one of the central issues in ethical theory. There is considerably less literature on the other viewpoints; in fact, the ethics of monetizing nonmonetary benefits and costs are on the frontiers of discussions within ethical theory. The conclusions of my analysis will be:

- In areas of environmental, safety, and health regulation, there may be many instances when a certain decision might be right even though the benefits of that decision do not outweigh the costs.

- There are a number of reasons to oppose efforts to put dollar values on nonmarketed benefits and costs, beyond the technical difficulties of doing so.

- Given the relative frequency of occasions in the areas of environmental, safety, and health regulation when it is not desirable to use a "benefits outweigh costs" test as a decision rule, and given the reasons to oppose the monetizing of nonmarketed benefits or of costs—a prerequisite for cost-benefit analysis—it is not justifiable to devote major resources to generate data to be used in cost-benefit calculations or to undertake an effort to "spread the gospel" of cost-benefit analysis further.

SHOULD BENEFITS OUTWEIGH COSTS?

How do we decide whether a given action is morally right or wrong and, assuming the desire to act morally, why it should be undertaken or refrained from? Like the Moliere character who spoke prose without knowing it, economists advocating the use of cost-benefit analysis for public decisions are philosophers without knowing it: the answer given by cost-benefit analysis, that actions should be undertaken so as to maximize net benefits, represents one of the classic answers given by moral philosophers. This is the doctrine of utilitarianism, associated with philosophers such as Bentham, Mill, and Sidgwick. Utilitarians argue that the right action under a given set of circumstances is the one that maximizes net satisfaction. To determine whether an action is right or wrong, all the positive consequences of the action in terms of human satisfaction should be totaled, and the act that maximizes attainment of satisfaction considered the right act.[1] The fact that the economists' answer is also the answer of one school of philosophers should not be surprising. Originally, economics was a branch of moral philosophy—Bentham and Sidgwick are famous not only among philosophers but are regarded by economists as their intellectual forebears. Only later on did economics separate from moral philosophy.

Before proceeding, the subtlety of the utilitarian position should be noted. For example, the positive and negative consequences of an act for the sum total of satisfaction in the world may go beyond the act's immediate consequences. A facile version of utilitarianism would give moral sanction to a lie, for instance, if the satisfaction an individual attained by telling the lie were greater than the suffering imposed on the victim of the lie.

Few utilitarians would agree, however. They would add to the list of negative consequences the effect of the one lie on the tendency of the person who lied to tell other lies, especially when those lies would produce less satisfaction for the liar than the dissatisfaction produced in others. They also would add the negative effects of the lie on general social respect for truth telling, a respect with many positive consequences. In addition, a negative consequence of a lie that some maintain must be added to the utilitarian calculation is the feeling of dissatisfaction produced in the individual (and perhaps in others) because, by telling a lie, one has "done the wrong thing." Correspondingly, in this view, among the positive consequences to be weighed into a utilitarian calculation of telling the truth is the satisfaction of "doing the right thing." This view rests on an error, however, because it assumes what it is the purpose of the calculation to determine—that telling the truth in the instance in question is indeed the right thing to do. For a utilitarian, there is nothing wrong about lying independent of its negative consequences (broadly regarded) for human satisfaction.

This last error is revealing, however, because it begins to suggest a critique of utilitarianism. Utilitarianism is an important and powerful moral doctrine. Few philosophers, including opponents of utilitarianism, would disagree that, for many actions, a utilitarian balancing of costs and benefits is an appropriate guide to moral choice. But it is probably fair to say that utilitarianism is a minority position among contemporary moral philosophers. It is indeed amazing that economists can proceed in unanimous endorsement of cost-benefit analysis as if unaware that in the discipline from which the conceptual framework for cost-benefit analysis arose, namely moral philosophy, this framework is, to put it mildly, highly controversial.

On the one hand, the notion that something is wrong unless its benefits outweigh its costs initially seems to be just common sense. On the other hand, the logical error discussed before indicates that our notion of certain things being right or wrong—such as telling a lie—predates our calculation of costs and benefits. Let us explore these contradictory intuitions with several examples.

Imagine the case of an old man in Nazi Germany who is hostile to the Nazi regime. He is wondering whether he should speak out against Hitler. If he speaks out, he will lose his pension. His action will do nothing to increase the chances that the Nazi regime will be overthrown since he is regarded as somewhat eccentric and nobody has ever consulted his views on political questions. Recall that any satisfaction from doing "the right thing" cannot be added to the benefits of speaking out because the purpose of the exercise is to determine whether speaking out is the right thing. The utilitarian calculation would determine that the benefits of speaking out, as the example is presented, would be nil. The cost would be the loss of the old man's pension. The costs of the action, therefore, would outweigh the benefits. By the utilitarian cost-benefit calculation, it would be morally wrong for the man to speak out.[2]

In another example two very close friends are on an Arctic expedition. One man becomes very sick in the snow and bitter cold, and he sinks quickly before anything can be done to help him. As he is dying, he asks his friend one thing, "Please, make me a solemn promise that 10 years from today you will come back to this spot and place a lighted candle here to remember me." The friend solemnly promises but does not tell a soul. Now, 10 years later, the friend must decide whether to fulfill his promise and return to the spot. It would be inconvenient for him to travel all the way back.

Since he told nobody, his failure to go would not affect the general social faith in promise keeping. And the incident was unique enough so that it is safe to assume that failure to go would not encourage the man to break other promises. Again, the costs of the act outweigh the benefits. A utilitarian would believe that it would be morally wrong to travel to the Arctic to light the candle.

A third example: a wave of thefts has hit a city. The police are having trouble finding any of the actual perpetrators. But they believe, correctly, that punishment of someone for theft will have some deterrent effect and will decrease the number of crimes. Unable to arrest any real perpetrator, the police chief and the prosecutor arrest a person whom they know to be innocent and, in cahoots with each other, fabricate a convincing case against him. The police chief and the prosecutor are about to retire, so the act will not affect their future actions. The fabrication is perfectly executed, and nobody finds out about it. In determining whether the act of framing the innocent man is morally correct, is the only question the one of whether the man's suffering from conviction and imprisonment will be greater than the suffering avoided among potential crime victims? A utilitarian would need to believe that is is morally right to punish the innocent man as long as it can be demonstrated that the suffering prevented outweighs his suffering.[3]

And a final example: imagine two worlds, each with the same sum total of happiness in them. In the first world, this particular total of happiness came about from a series of acts that included a number of lies and injustices. The sum total of happiness in this hypothetical world would consist of the immediate gross sum of happiness the acts created, minus any long-term unhappiness occasioned by lies or injustices. In the second world, the identical sum total of happiness was produced by a different series of acts, none of which involved lies or injustices. Are there any reasons to prefer the one world to the other? A utilitarian would believe that the choice between the two worlds is a matter of indifference.[4]

To those who believe that it would not be morally wrong for the old man to speak out in Nazi Germany or the man to venture to the Arctic to light a candle for his deceased friend, that it would not be morally right to convict the innocent man, or that the choice between the two worlds is not a matter of indifference, utilitarianism is insufficient as a moral view. Some acts whose costs are greater than their benefits may be morally right while some acts whose benefits are greater than their costs may be morally wrong.

This does not mean that the question of whether benefits are greater than costs is morally irrelevant. Few would claim such. Indeed, for a broad range of individual and social decisions, whether or not an act's benefits outweigh its costs is a sufficient question to ask. But not for all such decisions. There are situations in which certain duties—duties not to lie, break promises, or kill, for example—make an act wrong, even if the act would result in an excess of benefits over costs.[5] Another reason that an act might be wrong even though its benefits outweigh its costs is if that act violates someone's rights. We would not permit rape even if it could be demonstrated that the rapist derived enormous happiness from his act, while the victim only experienced a minor displeasure. We do not conduct cost-benefit analyses of freedom of speech or trial by jury. As the Steelworkers Union noted in a comment on the economic analysis of the Occupational Safety and Health Administration's (OSHA's) proposed regulation to reduce worker exposure to carcinogenic coke-oven emissions, the Emancipation Proclamation was not subjected to an inflationary impact statement. Similarly, the Bill of Rights is not subject to the Regulatory Analysis Review Group. The notion of human rights involves the idea that people may make certain claims to be allowed to act in certain ways, or to be treated in certain ways, even if the sum of benefits achieved thereby does not outweigh the sum of costs.[6] It is this view that lies behind statements like "workers have a right to a safe and healthy workplace," and behind the expectation that OSHA decisions will reflect that judgment.

In the most convincing versions of nonutilitarian (or deontological) ethics, various duties or rights are not absolute, but each has a *prima facie* moral validity such that, if duties or rights do not conflict, the morally right act is the act that reflects a duty or respects a right. If duties or rights do conflict, a moral judgment, based on deliberative reflection, must be made. One of the duties that deontological philosophers enumerate is the duty of beneficence (the duty to maximize happiness), which in effect incorporates all of utilitarianism by reference. Thus, a nonutilitarian, faced with conflicts between the results of cost-benefit analysis and the results of nonutility-based considerations, will need to undertake deliberative reflections. But additional elements in such deliberations, which cannot be reduced to whether benefits outweigh costs, exist. Indeed, depending on the moral importance we attach to the right or duty involved, questions of benefits and costs may, within wide ranges, become irrelevant to the outcome of the moral judgment.

In addition to questions of duties and rights, there is a final sort of question in which the issue of whether benefits outweigh costs should not determine moral judgment. I noted earlier that, for the common run of questions facing individuals and societies, it is possible to determine actions by calculating whether the benefits of the contemplated act outweigh the costs. Thus, one way for people to show the great importance or value attached to an issue is to say that decisions involving the issue should not be determined by cost-benefit calculations. This applies, I think, to the view many environmentalists have of decisions involving our natural environment. When decisions are being made about pollution levels that will harm certain vulnerable people—such as asthmatics or the elderly—while not harming others, issues of the rights of those people not to be sacrificed on the altar of somewhat higher living standards for the rest of us may be involved. Some environmentalists, in addition, speak of the "rights of nature" involved in environmental decisions. But more broadly than this, I believe many environmentalists object to the use of cost-benefit analysis for environmental decisions because the very act of using cost-benefit analysis for decisions about cleaning the air or water removes these questions from the realm of specially valued things where such calculations are not applicable.

USING A COMMON METRIC

In order for cost-benefit calculations to be performed, all costs and benefits must be expressed in a common metric, typically dollars. This creates an undisputed technical problem when placing a value on things not normally bought and sold on markets and to which no dollar price is attached. The most dramatic example of such things is human life itself, but many other benefits, such as peace and quiet, fresh-smelling air, swimmable rivers, or spectacular vistas, achieved or preserved by environmental policy also are not traded on markets.

Economists who use cost-benefit analysis have regarded the quest after dollar values for nonmarket things as a difficult challenge—and one joined with relish. Economists have tried to develop methods for imputing people's "willingness to pay" for nonmarket things. Essentially, the method involves searching for bundled goods that are traded on markets and whose price varies by whether or not they include a feature that is, by itself, not marketed. Thus, fresh air is not marketed but houses in different parts of Los Angeles that are similar except for the degree of smog are. Peace and quiet are not marketed but similar houses inside and outside airport flight paths are. The risk of death is not marketed but similar jobs that have different levels of risk are. Economists have made often ingenious efforts to impute dollar prices to nonmarketed things by calculating, for example, the premiums that homes in clean air areas attract over similar homes in dirty areas or of the premium of risky jobs over similar non-risky jobs. To the extent these efforts succeed, the ability to place nonmarket things into a common metric for the purpose of cost-benefit analysis succeeds.

Efforts to place nonmarket things into a common metric can be criticized on a number of technical grounds. First, the attempt to control and account for all the dimensions by which the bundled good can vary except for the nonmarketed thing may be difficult. More importantly, in a world where people vary in their preferences and the constraints to which they are subject, the dollar value imputed to nonmarket things that most people would wish to avoid will be lower than in a uniform world. This is because people with unusually weak aversion to these commodities or with unusually strong constraints on choice would be willing to take the bundled good in question at less of a discount than the average person. Thus, to use the property value discount of homes near airports as a measure of people's willingness to pay for quiet means to accept as a proxy for the rest of the population the behavior of those least sensitive to location, or of those susceptible to an agent's assurances that "it's not so bad." Similarly, to use the wage premiums accorded hazardous work as a measure of the value of life is to accept as proxies for the rest of us the choices of people who do not have many choices or who are exceptionally risk seeking.

A second problem is that the attempts of economists to measure people's "willingness to pay" for nonmarketed things do not differentiate between the price people will need to be paid to give up something to which they have a preexistent right and the price they would be willing to pay to gain something to which they enjoy no right. Thus, the analysis assumes no difference between how much a homeowner would need to be paid in order to give up an unobstructed mountain view that he or she already enjoys and how much the homeowner would be willing to pay to get an obstruction moved once it is already in place. Evidence suggests that most people would insist on being paid far more to assent to a worsening of their situation than they would be willing to pay to improve their situation. Such factors as habituation with the familiar and psychological attachments to that which people believe they enjoy a right account for the difference. This would create a circularity problem, for any attempt to use cost-benefit analysis would first have to determine whether to assign, for instance, the homeowner the right to an unobstructed mountain view. For the "willingness to pay" will be different depending on whether the right is initially assigned or not assigned. The value judgment about whether or not to assign the right must thus be made first.[7] (Actually, an analyst could assume assignment of the right to the person and determine how much he or she would need to be paid to give it up. This could set an upper bound on the benefit; if the costs were still greater, then by any test the costs of the measure outweigh the benefits.)

A third problem with placing nonmarket goods in a common metric is that the efforts economists make to impute willingness to pay all involve bundled goods exchanged in private transactions. People using figures garnered from such analysis to provide guidance for public decisions assume there is no difference between how people value certain things in private, individual transactions and how they would wish a social valuation of those same things to be made in public, collective decisions.

In assuming this, economists insidiously slip an important and controversial value judgment into their analysis—the view that there should be no difference between private, individual values and behavior, and the values and behavior displayed in public, social life. The view that public decisions should seek to mimic private, individual behavior grows naturally out of the highly individualistic microeconomic tradition. But it remains controversial nonetheless. An alternative view—one that enjoys wide resonance among many citizens—would be that public, social decisions provide an opportunity to give certain things a higher valuation than we choose, for one reason or another, to give these things in our private, individual activities.

Opponents of stricter regulation of health risks often argue that our daily risk-taking behavior indicates that we do not value life infinitely, and therefore our public decisions should not reflect the high value of life that proponents of strict regulation propose.

However, an alternative view is equally plausible. Precisely because we fail in everyday personal decisions, for whatever reasons, to give life the value we believe it should have, we wish our social decisions to display the reverence for life that we espouse but do not always show. By this view, people do not have fixed, unambiguous "preferences" which they express through private activities and which, therefore, should be expressed in public decisions. Rather, people may have what they themselves regard as "higher" and "lower" preferences. The latter may dominate in private decisions, but people may want the higher values to dominate in public decisions. For example, people may sometimes display racial prejudice but support anti-discrimination laws. They may buy a certain product after seeing a seductive ad but be skeptical enough of advertising to want the government to keep a close eye on it. In such cases, the use of private behavior to impute values for public decisions violates a view of citizen behavior that is deeply engrained in our democratic tradition. It is a view that denudes politics of any independent role in society, reducing it to a mechanistic recalculation based on private behavior.

Finally, putting a price on a nonmarket commodity and hence incorporating it into the market system may be opposed out of a fear that doing so will reduce the thing's perceived value. To place a price on the benefit of clean air, for example, may reduce the value of clean air. The act of cost-benefit analysis, thus, may affect the values of otherwise nonpriced benefits and costs.

Examples of the perceived cheapening of a thing's value by the very act of buying and selling it abound both in everyday life and language. The horror and disgust that accompany the idea of buying and selling human beings are based on the sense that this practice would dramatically diminish human worth. Epithets such as "he prostituted himself" and "he's a whore" applied as linguistic analogies to people who have sold something reflect the view that certain things should not be sold because doing so diminishes their value. One reason that pricing decreases something's perceived value is that nonmarket exchange often is associated with certain positively valued feelings that market exchange, using prices, is not. These may include feelings such as spontaneity and emotions that come from personal relationships.[8] If a good becomes disassociated from positively valued feelings because of market exchange, the good will lose its perceived value to the extent that those feelings are valued.

This loss can be seen clearly in instances when a thing may be transferred both by market and by nonmarket mechanisms. The willingness to pay for an apple in a store is less than the perceived value of the same apple presented as a gift by a friend or a stranger. The willingness to pay for sex bought from a prostitute is less than the perceived value of the sex consummating love. (Imagine the reaction if a practitioner of cost-benefit analysis computed the benefits of sex in our society based on the price of prostitute services.)

If a nonmarket sector is valued because of its connection with certain valued feelings, then any nonmarketed good is valued as a representative and part repository of values represented by the nonmarket sector. This status removed, the thing loses its repository character and, hence, part of its perceived value. This seems to be the case for the values placed on things in nature, such as pristine streams or undisturbed forests.

The second way that placing a market price decreases a thing's perceived value is by removing the possibility of proclaiming that the thing is "not for sale." The very statement that something is "not for sale" affirms, enhances, and protects a thing's value in a number of ways. Proclaiming a thing "not for sale" is a way of showing that the thing is valued for its own sake. By contrast, when a thing is sold for money, the thing sold is valued only instrumentally and not for its own sake. Furthermore, many goods sold are exchangeable for other goods of an unrelated nature. To state that something cannot be transferred in that way places it in an exceptional category.

If we do value something very highly, one way of stamping the thing with a cachet affirming its high value is to announce that it is "not for sale." Such an announcement does more, however, than just reflect—and affirm—a preexisting high valuation. It signals a thing's distinctive value to others and helps us exhort them to value the thing more highly than they otherwise might. And it also expresses our resolution to safeguard that distinctive value. To state that something is "not for sale" is thus also a source of value for that thing since, if a thing's value is easy to affirm, to exhort others to recognize, or to proclaim a desire to safeguard, it will be worth more than an otherwise similar thing without such abilities.

If something is declared "not for sale," a once-and-for-all judgment has been made of its special value. When something is priced, its perceived value is constantly being assessed, and a standing invitation exists to reconsider that original price. If people were constantly faced with questions such as "how much would you sell

your vote for if you could?" the perceived value of the freedom to
speak or the right to vote would soon become devastated, since, in
moments of weakness, people might decide that these values are not
worth so much after all. Something similar did in fact occur when
the slogan "better red than dead" was launched by some pacifists
during the Cold War. Critics pointed out that the very posing of this
stark choice—in effect, "would you really be willing to give up your
life in exchange for not living under communism?"—reduced the
value people attached to freedom and thus diminished resistance to
attacks on freedom.

Some things valued very highly are said to be "priceless," that
"no price is too high" for them, or that they have "infinite value."
This is not the case for all things considered "not for sale." Suppose
a daughter has some inexpensive candlesticks used many years earlier by her long-dead mother. She might well wish to proclaim that
they are not for sale as a way of affirming and protecting their value
to her. But she probably would not go so far as to use the word
"priceless" or "of infinite worth" to describe them. Such expressions
are reserved for a subset of things not for sale, such as life or health.

For an economist to state that something is "priceless" or that "no
price is too high" is to say that the economist would be willing to
trade off an infinite quantity of all other goods for one unit of priceless good, a situation that empirically appears highly unlikely.
Economists thus tend to scoff at talk of "pricelessness." What economists miss when they so scoff is the effect of the word "priceless"
on the thing to which the word is applied. The word "priceless" may
ring silly to an economist's ears, but to most people it is pregnant
with meaning.

The value-affirming and value-protecting functions cannot be
bestowed to expressions that merely denote attribution of a determinate, albeit high, valuation. John F. Kennedy in his inaugural address proclaimed that the nation was ready to "pay any price (and)
bear any burden . . . to assure the survival and the success of liberty." Had he stated instead (as most economists probably would
have preferred) that we were willing to "pay a high price" or "bear a
large burden" for liberty, the statement would have rung hollow.[9]

CONCLUSION

An objection that advocates of cost-benefit analysis might well
make to the preceding argument should be considered. I noted ear-

lier that, when various nonutility-based duties or rights conflict with maximization of utility, it is necessary to make a deliberative judgment about what act is finally right. I also argued earlier that the search for commensurability might not always be a desirable one, that the attempt to go beyond expressing benefits in terms of, say, lives saved and costs in terms of dollars is not something devoutly to be wished.

In situations involving things not expressed in a common metric—where a lie is on one side and a certain amount of happiness on the other, or lives on one side and dollars on the other—advocates of cost-benefit analysis frequently argue that people making judgments "in effect" perform cost-benefit calculations anyway. If government regulators promulgate a regulation that saves 100 lives at a cost of $1 billion, they are "in effect" valuing a life at a minimum of $10 million, whether or not they say that they are willing to place a dollar value on a human life. Since, in this view, cost-benefit analysis "in effect" is inevitable, it might as well be made specific.

This argument misconstrues the real difference in the reasoning processes involved. In cost-benefit analysis, equivalencies are established in advance as one of the raw materials for calculation. We determine costs and benefits, we determine equivalencies (various costs and benefits are put into a common metric), and then we tote things up—waiting, as it were, with bated breath for the results of the calculation. The outcome is determined by the arithmetic; if the outcome is a close call, we do not know how it will turn out until the calculation is finished. In the kind of deliberative judgment that is performed without a common metric—rights and utility, dollars and lives—there is no establishing equivalencies or calculations. The equivalencies that the decision maker, according to this argument, "in effect" uses, are not aids to the decision process. In fact, the decision maker might not even be aware of what the "in effect" equivalencies are, at least before they are revealed to him afterwards by someone pointing out what he or she had "in effect" done. The decision maker would see him or herself as simply having made a deliberative judgment; the "in effect" equivalency number did not play a causal role in the decision but at most merely reflects it.[10] Given this, the argument against making the process explicit is the one advanced earlier in the discussion of problems with putting specific quantified values on things that are not normally quantified—that the very act of doing so may reduce the value of such things.

My own judgment, in conclusion, is that modest efforts to assess levels of benefits and costs are justified, although I do not believe that government agencies ought give a cachet to efforts to put dollar prices on nonmarket things. I do not believe that the cry "we need more cost-benefit analysis in regulation" is, on the whole, justified. If sensitivity about regulatory costs were sufficiently primitive among regulatory officials to not even provide acceptable raw material for deliberative judgments (even of a nonstrictly cost-benefit nature), this conclusion might be different. But this does not, it seems, reflect the current reality of the regulatory environment. The danger now would seem to come more from the other side.

Notes

1. For accounts of utilitarianism and its critics, see any standard textbook in ethical theory, such as Richard Brandt, *Ethical Theory* (Englewood Cliffs: Prentice Hall, 1959), Ch. 15-17; or William Frankena, *Ethics* (Englewood Cliffs: Prentice Hall, 1973). See also J.J.C. Smart and Bernard Williams, *Utilitarianism: For and Against* (Cambridge: Cambridge University Press, 1973).

2. This example is adapted from Thomas E. Hill, Jr. "Symbolic Protest and Calculated Silence," *Philosophy and Public Affairs*, 9 (Fall 1979), p. 84.

3. This example is adapted from Brandt, *op. cit.*, p. 494.

4. This example is somewhat analogous to one found in G.E. Moore, *Principia Ethica* (Cambridge: Cambridge University Press, 1903), pp. 84-5.

5. The independent status of such duties as moral concepts—independent, that is, of the question of utility maximization—may be regarded as an unanalyzable ultimate moral concept, similar as an ultimate concept to the concept that maximizing satisfaction is right. In other words, asking "why is lying wrong?"cannot be answered more satisfactorily than the question, "why is making someone unhappy wrong?"

6. For more on rights, see for instance, Ronald Dorkin, *Taking Rights Seriously* (Cambridge: Harvard University Press, 1977), particularly Ch. 6-7, and A.I. Melden (editor), *Human Rights* (Belmont, California: Wadsworth Publishing, 1970).

7. For a further discussion, see Mark Kelman, "Consumption Theory, Production Theory, and Ideology in the Coase Theorem" *Southern California Law Review*, 52 (March 1979).

8. For a further discussion, see Steven Kelman, "Economic Incentives and Environmental Policy: Politics, Philosophy, Ideology" (manuscript, 1980), pp. 85-118.

9. For a more detailed discussion, see *Ibid.*, pp. 119-29.

10. In these circumstances, the value of the "in effect" equivalency number would be for use in future decisions, to achieve "consistency." But the decision maker might be uneasy about applying the results of one deliberation automatically to other deliberations, either out of an unwillingness to cast deliberative judgment in stone or out of a belief that different circumstances may not show enough in common.

Part IV
CONCLUSION

8/EXCERPTS

Conference Discussion Highlights

The preceding articles on the Illinois economic impact assessment program and on the methods, politics, and ethics of cost-benefit analysis were supplemented, at the Chicago conference, by audience discussions and by the remarks of additional speakers featured at the meeting.* This compilation highlights some of the major issues addressed in these exchanges.

UNCERTAINTY, BIAS, AND ERROR

While advocating the use of cost-benefit analysis, Messrs. Hurter, Tolley, and Fabian recognize in their essay the limits of the technique and plead for patience while methods are improved. Three of the methodological issues addressed at the Chicago conference included the magnitude of error in cost-benefit analysis, the possible bias in this technique against future generations, and the usefulness of cost-benefit analyses in which gains and losses are quantified but not translated into dollar terms.

QUESTION: Are there so many opportunities for error in cost-benefit analysis that it will not be an aid in decision making?
Former EPA Administrator Douglas Costle discussed several computational difficulties in cost-benefit analysis and stressed that economic calculations cannot and should not replace social policy judgments in public decisions:

---

* Other featured speakers included: Frank Beal, Director of the Illinois Institute of Natural Resources; Douglas Costle, former Administrator of the U.S. Environmental Protection Agency; David Doniger, Senior Project Attorney, Natural Resources Defense Council; A. Myrick Freeman, Professor of Economics, Bowdoin College; Paul Freeman, former Special Assistant to the Director, National Commission on Air Quality; Lewis Perl, Senior Vice President, National Economic Research Associates; and Paul Portney, Senior Fellow, Resources for the Future.

[The value of cost-benefit analysis is limited,]...and unless we recognize its shortcomings, we are likely to force a superficial quantification on issues that cannot be wholly grasped by the reassuringly precise embrace of numbers ....[T]he result will not only be bad cost-benefit analysis, but bad decisions....

Society must make some cold-eyed calculation about how much it can afford to preserve a human life....[But] cost-benefit analysis, no matter how precise, cannot replace social policy judgments. It can allow us to order the evidence, fragmentary though it may be, in a more rational way. Used properly, it can illuminate public decisions. Used improperly it can obfuscate them for self-serving purposes. What such analysis can do is to help produce refined and explicit economic comparisons so that the policy maker sees more clearly the dimensions of the decision before him....

We cannot substitute the sophisticated, mechanical business of piling numbers on either side of a balance for the agonizing process of making fallible inescapable human judgments. For such judgments are at one in the same time a dilemma and the glory of any society that aspires to be just.

Dr. Lewis Perl contended that cost-benefit analysis would help reduce some of the uncertainty that Mr. Costle stated was inherent in environmental decision making, and that the technique was no more subject to abuse than any other technical or economic calculation that might be used in a decision. He stressed that analytical uncertainties were attributable more to the epidemiological and meteorological data fed into the analysis than to the technique itself:

Most cost-benefit analysts, myself included, have a very similar view of the usefulness and desirability of the technique. Each of us tends to feel that our own analyses represent thoughtful, balanced assessments that are essential to making intelligent and informed policy choices. However, everyone else's analyses are a heady brew of bad data, bad theory, witchcraft, and value judgments, which are either too uncertain to guide policy makers at all, or are designed to lead or mislead the policy maker into doing what the analyst thinks is best. I think that last description aptly summarizes Doug Costle's views last night....I still come to the conclusion that for all its flaws, cost-benefit analysis represents the only viable methodology for evaluating environmental regulations and developing intelligent alternative regulations....

[W]hy do I still think that there's any worth in this technique? First, most of the uncertainties in the literature are really not uncertainties in the technique; they're uncertainties in the data bases, most of which, I think, are resolvable on the basis of additional research and in some cases not a lot of additional research.... Many of the differences among the existing studies result because people use slightly different [research] methods, and many of these differences can be resolved. Given the magnitude of the money that we're spending on environmental programs... surely we can afford a few million dollars to resolve some of the remaining uncertainties....

The second point I would make is when we get all done with that, there will inevitably be a lot of uncertainty left, far less than exists now....But I think the thing that one ought to see is that uncertainty is inherent in the decision-making process itself and really has nothing to do with cost-benefit analysis.... It seems to me to argue, as Mr. Costle did last night, that the uncertainties are a basis of the choice between administrative discretion and the use of [cost-benefit] techniques really makes no sense at all. Both administrative discretion and the use of these techniques have uncertainties in them and they're the same uncertainties. At some point you're going to come to the conclusion that you really don't know exactly what the effect of air pollution is on cancer. And if there's latency in the problem you won't know for years. But you are still going to make a decision to control a little bit more or to control a little bit less, and in making that decision, you are going to be balancing the possibility that there are great risks against the possibility that there are limited risks. That's the nature of the decision-making process. [When two authors give you competing assessments of risks, making] your own judgments about which author you think is giving you the straight scoop is more sensible than just guessing [about the desirable level of control].

The last issue is... cheating. If there's a lot of money at stake... then people are going to... inevitably slant the results to favor the conclusion they favor, and that's true on either side of the issue. It seems to me that's equally true of any other technique you employ. If you say everything should be determined on the basis of what is technologically feasible, then industry will come in and argue that nothing is technologically feasible. If you say it should all be determined on whether you're going to bankrupt the industry, then everyone will come in and cry to you about how this legislation is going to bankrupt me. If you tell them everything shall be determined on the balance of costs and benefits, then people who don't want to do it will tell you the costs are too high and the benefits are low, and people who want you to do it will say the benefits are high and the costs are low. But that is the role of the administrator, that is, to take all of the cost-benefit literature, and balance it, and say "Well, I thought that study was poor because they were lying about the costs or the benefits," and "I thought that was a good study," and do your own. That is precisely the role of environmental administrators—to take the evidence and weigh it and make a decision.

David Doniger had been asked to deliver the "no" statement in a forum on the question "Should cost-benefit analysis be mandatory for all major federal environmental regulations?" He cited a situation where cost-benefit analysis might not be very helpful to decision makers:

> [In some situations] the health data or environmental effects data may not be in anybody's hands because the subjects are so much on the frontiers of knowledge. I think that even if you pour a great deal of money into solving those kinds of problems, it would take a very long time and you'd still end up with such uncertainties in the data that on any close question, *data* is not going to resolve the controversy or tell you what kind of a trade-off you should make....

> [One] area where that is definitely the case is... carcinogenicity, where the available plausible methods for modeling what the risks are at the relevant levels of exposure are so uncertain that they can differ from one another by factors of *five million times.* It doesn't do much except slow the regulation process to encourage industry to come in with its model, public interest groups to come in with their model, and the agency to come in with its model too....

QUESTION: Is the methodology of cost-benefit analysis inherently biased against future generations?

Dr. Devra Lee Davis of the Environmental Law Institute inquired whether, because of the uncertainties discussed by Messrs. Costle, Perl, and Doniger, cost-benefit analysis is inherently biased against future generations:

> [H]ow do we justify and rationalize decisions where we know that we are missing information that may well affect future generations?... in the cases of Tris or saccharin or vinyl chloride..., there is toxicological and epidemiological evidence that the intergenerational irreversible genetic risks of these substances may be great. In light of that, it seems to me to underregulate poses a far greater public health risk than overregulation.

Dr. Perl responded:

> I think that the intergenerational impact issue exists not only on the adverse consequences of environmental damage but on the adverse consequences of the controls of environmental damage. That is, we are going to hand on to the next generation an environment which is going to be with them; we are also going to hand on to them an economic base which is going to be with them, and both of these things are going to determine in a very profound way their welfare.... I think that the only easy thing you can say about the intergenerational problem is that it is not one which quite obviously says we should have more stringent regulations because we're protecting not only ourselves but our children and our grandchildren. It just makes the problem more complicated. We're protecting them or

harming them, whichever action we take, and I don't see any convincing evidence that the decision is biased one way or the other by looking only at this generation. But I do know that if I try to look at the next generation, since I'm confused as it is, that I've just made the problem impossible. So I think that for those people who think that's an important part of the problem, you really have to say something more than what you just said. You have to be able to present convincing evidence, even modestly convincing evidence, that there are intergenerational problems on the environmental side, but no intergenerational problems on the economic side, or no balancing problems.

Dr. Kevin Croke also responded to Dr. Davis' question, and he acknowledged the difficulty policy analysts have with intergenerational impacts:

I think the intergenerational problem is... so scary or so big it's almost hard to touch or people don't want to touch it.... I think it was Alvin Weinberg that suggested a nuclear priesthood that would be established to look after our nuclear waste for hundreds and hundreds and thousands of years. The thought of Father Radium looking after our future is a little bit more than a benefit-cost analyst would like to think about. I think the intergenerational problem will have to bring forth some new facets of analysis in benefit-cost calculations.... It's so far in the future that conventional discounting type analysis becomes questionable....

QUESTION: Does cost-benefit analysis require translation of all or most impacts into dollars in order to be useful to decision makers?

Several speakers, including some of those already quoted, emphasized the difficulty of attaching dollar values to the gains and losses from regulation, but many of them also stressed that efforts at nonmonetized quantification might nevertheless be useful for purposes of ordering data, for setting priorities, and for otherwise adding to the information base on which decisions rest. This point of view is embodied in the set of remarks of Dr. Paul Portney, who was asked to deliver the "yes" statement in a forum on making cost-benefit analysis mandatory for all major federal environmental regulations. Portney also addressed the bias and cheating questions:

Now before I indicate why I believe that cost-benefit analysis should be required to accompany all major federal environmental regulations, let me ask you to listen carefully to what I am not supporting here....

I am *not* saying that each and every effect of an environmental or other kind of regulation should be quantified in numbers, then translated into dollars, and placed on an even footing with every other effect of regulation. It sometimes cannot be done, and there is nothing in cost-benefit analysis that requires that it be done. That is to say, there is nothing in cost-benefit analysis that says that every last effect must be translated into dollars and placed on that single scale.

Next, I am *not* saying that a regulation should be approved if and only if the ratio of benefits to costs is greater than one, or that a rule should be opposed if the ratio of benefits to costs is less than one. [Cost-benefit ratios] are not rules that can determine in the absence of other information whether regulations should be issued or not. There are a number of very other important criteria that we must consider at the same time we consider economic efficiency. Among these others quite obviously [is] equity, and that is equity between income groups, between geographical regions, and between generations.... In addition, any administrator worth his or her salt has to take into account things like political feasibility, [the] implementability of various regulations....

I think [cost-benefit analysis] is one of the tools that can indicate to us where we have gone too far, where our zeal has been too great, and, in other areas, where we may be underregulating. And there is nothing inherent in cost-benefit analysis that makes it anti-environmental.... [The CEQ benefits study] indicated that it appears that the benefits associated with the Clean Air Act, on a take-or-leave-it basis, may well exceed the costs of the act... I believe we can meet existing environmental goals and standards for considerably less money than we're now spending... and I favor benefit-cost analysis because... I think it's the best method we have now to find cheaper ways to meet those standards. It forces a clear scrutinization of alternatives and it helps us discover ways to meet standards for less, which we're going to have to do if we don't want to see those standards knocked down and reduced still further....

[Second], since everyone has made this point today, let me only throw in with all of those who have said as long as it's being done implicitly, one value of cost-benefit analysis is that it points out to the administrator the value that he or she is placing on lives.... [I]t's not some Machiavellian plot by economists to monetize human lives or other kinds of incommensurables; it's a concrete way to ensure that we actually do produce as many of the desired effects for the given expenditure of dollars as we possibly can. And certainly no one can argue with the point that if EPA is going to provide safety at our expense, then they ought to provide as much safety as possible for the dollars that we have to spend for those programs....

Finally, I don't accept the view that the occasional and sometimes egregious misuse of cost-benefit analysis is a justification for throwing it out, any more than I would say that the occasional misuse of or mayhem arising from hammers or chainsaws are justifications for banning them from the market. Because a tool is occasionally misused does not mean that we want to deprive ourselves of all uses of it.

POLITICS

In his essay on the politics of cost-benefit analysis, Richard N.L. Andrews notes that cost-benefit analysis, properly used, can improve some decisions but, improperly used, it may do the opposite. The many caveats Andrews and others offer suggest that steps should be taken to identify when cost-benefit analysis might be most and least useful and when it might be given most and least weight. This, in essence, is a political endeavor that takes account of methodological limitations: institutions and administrative decision processes must be structured to minimize abuses of this method.

Two political issues addressed at the Chicago conference were the desirability of cost-benefit analysis relative to other proposed decision strategies, and the desirability of having costs considered in setting ambient standards under the Clean Air Act.

QUESTION: If cost-benefit analysis is rejected for environmental decision making, because of concern about uncertainties and abuse, will this encourage other analytical or institutional approaches to promote "balance?" Will these others be less manageable and, perhaps, more perverse?

Paul Portney:

Let me indicate a final and what may sound like a Draconian reason why I believe that cost-benefit analysis is important and should be mandatory in accompanying federal environmental regulations, and that is this: if you don't like it, you ought to see what's waiting in the wings to replace it. I'll tick off three supposed substitutes, which are designed to remedy the lack of analysis in environmental regulation. First, the legislative veto, which has already been affixed to EPA pesticide regulations and to regulations from the Federal Trade Commission. This would enable one or two Houses of Congress, depending on the particular version, to veto any environmental or other kind of regulation that they don't like within 30 days of promulgation. Now this would have the effect of making their staffs sort of duplicate regulatory agencies, so that every single regulation issued by the EPA or another agency would also have to be scrutinized by the Congressional staffs so that they could recommend to their representative whether he or she ought to vote to veto it or not. In other words, we'll go through a whole second iteration on this process, to little good effect I believe.

The second alternative to better use of cost-benefit analysis in current regulation is the so-called Bumpers amendment, expanding judicial review of current regulations. This would have the effect of directing the courts to no longer presume that regulations offered by regulatory agencies are valid unless demonstrated otherwise. You could say in effect that the court presumes that we start with a clean slate, that maybe the regulation is okay and maybe it's not, and we shift all of the burden of decision making onto judges, who, I would argue, are even less qualified than you may believe the people who run the regulatory agencies in Washington are [to make those decisions]. I certainly don't think that judges are more qualified.... There's enough delay in the court system now without throwing still a greater burden on their shoulders as the Bumpers amendment or other proposals for judicial review will do.

The final substitute to the increased use of cost-benefit analysis in regulation is the regulatory budget, which each year would say that EPA [and other agencies] can impose no more than x dollars in compliance costs on the private sector.... In other words, you would put a limit on the costs they could impose on the private sector, in the same way we put a limit on [other ways] the agency decides to spend its money. And as I say, if you don't like cost-benefit analysis and view it as a threat to regulation, you ain't seen nothing yet.

U.S. EPA's David Schnare echoed Portney's comments:

[I]f we don't do benefit-cost analysis to provide us some hedge on uncertainties and unknowabilities, what will we be stuck with? I think we'll be stuck with some very unhappy and unfortunate ways to capture the worst of politics rather than the best of it. Inevitably, any tool that's available is going to be politicized, and the question is which can be politicized the least and I suspect that that might well be cost-benefit analysis.

David Doniger was troubled by both sets of remarks:

I'd like to respond to that, and to Paul's suggestion that there are worse things around the corner. I agree that the three things he listed are all terrible. However, I'm not sure what the best strategy is for avoiding getting stuck with all four. You run a risk of getting stuck with all four, if you accept the first. And so I'm not sure, as purely political judgment, that we are incorrect if we wish to draw the line here [and not accept] cost-benefit analysis as a mandatory requirement....

I won't repeat too much of what has been said about the weaknesses of cost-benefit analysis.... I don't think [it takes much] to oppose highly quantitative, highly monetized cost-benefit analysis. Neither Paul Portney nor many of the other speakers here today stands for *that* sort of analysis. But there are many out there, in the courts, in Congress, and the newspapers who are trying to sell what I think is so vast an oversimplification that it amounts to a big lie: that there are ways to objectively quantify and put dollar signs on the things that are at stake in health and environmental regulation. Now I don't think it takes too much discussion today... to dispute that. But it is important to recognize that there are lots of people out there who, either out of naivete or out of hidden motives, don't know that or admit it, and it's necessary to remain opposed to that school of analysis....

[I cannot freely abandon] the idea that life is something you don't compromise for any purpose. I realize the problems with that position, but it's also something pretty deep in our tradition, as Steve Kelman pointed out, and very valuable for us to maintain. I reconcile that with the need to "balance" by drawing a distinction. [On the one hand, there are] those whose goal it is eventually to eliminate... disease to the greatest extent [possible]. Those people realize of course that it can't be done right away, that there are many pressing conflicting needs, and that, as a kind of a compromise with both technical and political reality, you must balance. That's the kind of person I suppose I am.

There are others, however, who elevate balancing and compromise to being a high goal in itself.

Over time, you continue to work towards that goal of zero risk where you can get it, of safety where you can get it, if you hold the view that I'm subscribing to. If you hold the other view, however, you could find situations where risks are now very low, but are explicitly permitted to increase, because a higher level—say of cancer—has been declared acceptable. We find that such people would consider it okay to degrade some area of life by adding new risks to it so long as they don't exceed that acceptable risk threshold. [I'm proposing here] a kind of prevention of significant deterioration in the risk levels we face in areas where we're now relatively safe.

QUESTION: How are costs taken into consideration in setting national ambient air quality standards under the Clean Air Act and in establishing deadlines for achieving them, and how should costs be taken into account?

The costs of implementing the Clean Air Act have been hotly debated, and some have suggested that cost-benefit analysis be used in setting national ambient air quality standards. David Doniger described the rationale for leaving costs out of the standard-setting process, at least in theory:

The ambient standards are supposed to be set with respect to health factors only, in theory. The danger that I see in making cost-benefit analysis a requirement in the setting of those standards is quality. When you set the standards you have health data, which is not perfect by any means, but you have almost no data on most of the costs for many industries in the states, on many different combinations of cleanup, or on technical innovations that can possibly reduce costs. Everyone who will be paying those costs has an interest in stating what their maximum might be.

The purpose of leaving costs out of the balance [at the standard setting stage], beyond affirming that these standards should say what air is healthy to breathe, is to put the states or the industries within states to the test of figuring out what methods of compliance are available... what's the least costly alternative. And you'll find, I think, a great deal more innovation, a great deal more pursuit of less costly alternatives if you leave the analysis of costs until later; it's a little bit like a game of chicken where you have to see who's going to jump first. Unfortunately, Congress tends to jump first—before the industries, in many cases—and the deadlines get postponed. But if you brought cost analysis right up to the stage of setting the standards, and then balanced costs and benefits there, you would find the standards would be a great deal weaker and many opportunities for innovation, for pressing institutions both private and public, to change the things that they're doing that generate pollution, would be lost....

I think the proper answer to an industry-sponsored analysis of what a standard will cost is to say you can't possibly know, particularly if we're just starting to control that substance for the first time. And we can't possibly know either. So we're not going to engage in a game of speculating about what the costs will be until there's been some effort to innovate, which can only be motivated under the real threat of deadlines and penalties, to figure out what can be done. Maybe after a while we can get some sense of what it has cost, but the problem is that for as long as people believe there is an escape valve or a reconsideration coming up, they have an incentive to put things off rather than make the hard choices.

There are some situations in which the proper answer is: "no one can do that sort of analysis now."

Paul Freeman, of the National Commission on Air Quality, echoed some of Doniger's views, yet he also recognized that costs creep into the standard-setting process:

Implicit in the act's provisions with respect to standard-setting is the idea that there exist threshold levels of exposure, that if pollution is present but in a quantity below the threshold, there will be no serious health and welfare effects. Some of the recent scientific findings tell us this may be nothing more than wishful thinking. If these new findings are accurate, the implication is clear. In order to truly protect the most sensitive parts of the population with an adequate margin of safety, as the act requires, EPA would have to set the standards at zero. EPA has not done this and Congress has acquiesced....

Why has EPA been able to do this? One reason is the limited and conflicting results of medical research. The other more important reason is obvious. If standards were set at zero, costs would be unacceptably high....

The point is, at least implicitly, at least informally—costs are considered. Even, I would argue, in establishing the supposedly solely health-based standards. This is not to say the costs should not be considered more formally or differently, but to say that the idea that costs are totally ignored in standard-setting is false....

Another part of the act often singled out for criticism is that related to deadlines for meeting the ambient standards.... The history of the act includes a continued willingness on the part of Congress to grant extensions of various deadlines, if they're found to be unattainable or unduly burdensome. The deadlines in the act are the result of ar least an implicit—albeit crudely performed—consideration of costs and benefits, which reflects... the twofold objective of Congress in this area. First, set deadlines far enough into the future so that the country can be given adequate time to meet them; and second, to force areas which otherwise might be inclined to delay to instead begin taking some reasonably progressive steps immediately.

ETHICS

Steven Kelman addressed the ethics issue at length, and it was touched on by many other speakers at the Chicago conference. One exchange in particular underscored Kelman's principal point.

A participant commented:

You talked about buying a friend.... When it comes to friendship, isn't there not the buying of friendship in the sense of decisions to invest time with other people? You don't buy it with money, but how do you develop friendships except by the investment of time with a person and sharing experiences over time and things like that?

Kelman responded:

I'd suggest most people do not conceptualize befriending other people in terms of investment of time that is expected to yield a stream of benefits discounted to present value. There are economists... who have tried to analyze things such as friendship in terms of investment of time and other kinds of quasi-economic reasoning. I would suggest most people don't do that, and I would suggest that a society where most people did that would be a society where friendship had lost some of its value as a social relationship.

POLITICS, ETHICS, AND METHODS IN THE ILLINOIS PROGRAM

The essay by Kevin Croke and Niels Herlevsen focused on some important administrative issues raised by the Illinois economic impact assessment program. These merit attention by other states considering economic impact assessment programs. Frank Beal, Director of the Illinois Institute of Natural Resources, addressed the Chicago meeting and focused less on administrative issues and more on the political, ethical, and methodological questions that had been raised by other speakers:

[I]t is clear that the issues raised at this conference do not lend themselves to easy resolution.... Let me tell you some of the reasons why [the Illinois program] is successful or at least moving in the right direction.... We have, I think, managed to avoid or probably more accurately sidestep many of the constroversial issues raised in this conference. In the first place, it should be noted that we do not conduct rigid cost-benefit analyses; we usually don't attempt to place a price on life...; therefore we would not... for the most part assemble a single cost-benefit ratio number. We draw people's attention to the potential benefits of these so-called priceless goods, but we normally don't price them ourselves.

The second reason why I think the program is successful... is that the agency that proposes or prepares the economic statement is not the agency that must decide [on an] environmental regulation.... In other words, the economic statement is not determinate; the Board can [and does] take into account numerous other variables besides the economic costs and benefits.... However, as Kevin Croke pointed out, there is a loss in that separation. [But the separation should continue.]

Third, the whole process doesn't cost much; maybe $300,000 to $500,000 a year. Given the immense cost of complying with environmental regulations, and the equally large benefits, [that part of the] tax dollar is not particularly large. It is my opinion that all parties to the process... are in fact all the more sensitive to the costs and benefits of regulation. While it is generally acknowledged that the business community supported the Illinois program in the hope of demonstrating the high costs and perhaps the unreasonably high costs of complying with regulations, and the environmental community opposed the program out of fear that it would be the opening skirmish in a battle to destroy the environmental movement, I think it's fair to say the results have not been nearly so dramatic. However, I do believe that more care goes into drafting of proposed regulations in this state, so that they are in fact sensitive to the costs of compliance. I also believe the program has had a salutory effect of demonstrating quite convincingly that there are substantial benefits no matter how we measure them, to be gained from environmental regulation....

[I was quite struck] by Mr. Kelman's argument about debasing the quality of life by attempting the very effort of putting a pricetag on it.... Nonetheless, I think I have a responsibility to share the information that I have available. That responsibility, of course, entails a concern for the manner in which the information is presented. In doing so, I understand that I cannot reduce an infinitely complex problem into a series of 8 or 10 facts or figures, and certainly not into a single cost-benefit ratio. To make no effort to analyze the costs and benefits of public policy would be to demonstrate a lack of faith in our political leaders and our political system. It is an issue I think Mr. Andrews spoke to very well; I concurred with his analysis.... If we are to ask our political leaders to make what are in fact life and death decisions, and we recognize them as such, then I think it is our responsibility to provide those same leaders with the best possible information we have and to maintain our confidence that those leaders can understand the information for what it is: an abstraction of the real world that must be assimilated and integrated into a more complex personal and political decision-making structure.

9/CONCLUSION

Toward Productive Dialogue

Daniel Swartzman

This book has examined the current use of cost-benefit analysis in Illinois and in the federal government. It has analyzed in some detail the sources of controversy regarding the application of cost-benefit analysis to environmental regulations, and it has referenced numerous other sources that develop further the pros and cons of the issue.[1]

Where should participants in the debate go from here, especially those who have taken firm positions on this issue? We can continue engaging in fruitless and frustrating dialogues typified by the dialogue that introduced Part III of this book. Or we can fall back, regroup, and prepare to "duke it out" before state legislatures and Congress, as is being done on Capitol Hill during the reauthorization of the Clean Air Act.

Or maybe we can pursue a middle course between rhetorical stalemate and political battle. Maybe we can decide through productive dialogue whether or how to use cost-benefit analysis in environmental regulation. This chapter explores that possibility by posing the following questions:

- Can we find out how the participants in policy making believe these controversies should be resolved?

- Why should anyone want to use cost-benefit analysis for environmental regulations?

- How might we wish to control the use of cost-benefit analysis, given its widely recognized limitations?

- What issues remain to be resolved before the use of cost-benefit analysis might be openly agreed upon?

- Why should we try to achieve consensus on this controversy?

ATTITUDES OF POLICY-MAKING PARTICIPANTS

Much of the current discussion of cost-benefit analysis in environmental regulation occurs among economists, political scientists, lawyers, engineers, and the politicians who rely on these professions for advice. Occasionally, we can find a stray media report[2] or an editorial[3] in a major newspaper, but rarely is cost-benefit analysis, *per se*, a headline-grabbing subject in papers other than those such as the *Los Angeles Times* or *The Washington Post*.

Is it possible that these participants in the policy-making process share certain attitudes towards the use of cost-benefit analysis in environmental decisions? On what do they agree, and on what do they disagree? Such information is necessary as a starting point for productive dialogue.

As a first attempt to see whether this type of information can be gathered and used, a questionnaire was administered at the conference that gave rise to this book. The audience was asked to express agreement or disagreement with 15 statements about the use of cost-benefit analysis in environmental regulations. They also were asked to indicate, among other things, their principal occupation or volunteer affiliation. Their responses are summarized in Table 1.

Admittedly, the survey design was far from ideal.[4] This protocol however, had some strengths for exploring whether we can measure directly the attitudes of policy-making participants toward cost-benefit analysis. The test population represented a diverse group of concerned individuals, professional and nonprofessional people working for a variety of organizations. The sample group was very knowledgeable about environmental problems and regulatory strategies that address them. By and large, they are strongly committed to environmental concerns and probably are leaders among their peers. Most importantly, this survey represents a significant first step toward measuring the sources and the depth of the controversy over cost-benefit analysis.

To permit statistical analyses of survey results, several categories of responses were collapsed. "Agree" and "strongly agree" responses were combined, as were "disagree" and "strongly disagree." The "business/industry" and "consultant" categories also were collapsed, since most of the consultants contract with business and industry, and the responses from the two groups tended to be similar. "Environmental group staff/volunteers" had responses very similar to the "environmental regulators," so these two categories were collapsed as well.

Four patterns of responses emerged from this consolidation: (1) general disagreement regarding a statement; (2) disagreement between industry representatives and consultants on the one hand and environmentalists and environmental regulators on the other; (3) agreement, with some groups agreeing less strongly than others; and (4) general agreement.

Looking at the results for each statement separately indicates the possible fruitfulness of dialogue. For instance, extreme positions (statements 2 and 14) were rejected roundly by all the participants, regardless of affiliation. Productive dialogue is more likely when people's positions are not polarized.

There were a number of statements about the benefits of cost-benefit analysis with which all the participants agreed, although environmentalists and regulators supported these statements less strongly. The participants agreed that cost-benefit analysis could be used to promote more cost-effective regulations (statement 12), that the analysis of costs and benefits was part of a sound policy to use scarce resources wisely (statement 8), and that cost-benefit analysis likely could improve decisions (statement 7).

But the participants also strongly agreed with two statements (5 and 9) about the limits of cost-benefit analysis: that cost-benefit analyses usually are biased to support the views of their sponsors and that cost-benefit analyses are not simple analogs to the private decisions of individuals.

These agreements on the strengths and limits of cost-benefit analysis are encouraging; they may provide a basis for dialogue that clarifies disagreements and identifies additional agreements.

As might have been expected, there were areas of strong disagreement. On the basic question (statement 1) of whether we need more cost-benefit analysis because we are spending too much for too little benefit, participants exhibited strong, statistically significant, disagreement.[5] On three statements (4, 11, and 13) that covered the methods, ethics, and politics of cost-benefit analysis, the participants split between business/industry and consultants versus environmentalists and environmental regulators. Participants disagreed as to whether cost-benefit analysis relies on too many questionable assumptions and leaps of judgment (statement 13).[6] They also disagreed strongly on whether placing a dollar value on

TABLE 1

Selected Responses of Conference Participants on Opinion Survey*

QUESTIONS	Business/Industry and Consultant		Environmental Group Staff/Volunteer and Environmental Regulator		TOTAL
	AGREE	DISAGREE	AGREE	DISAGREE	
1. More analysis of costs and benefits of environmental rules is needed because we are spending too much money for too little benefit.	12	5	6	31	54
2. Analysis of costs and benefits of environmental rules should be discouraged because this will inevitably weaken such rules.	1	16	5	33	55
3. Analysis of costs and benefits of environmental rules should be encouraged because benefits of most rules likely outweigh their costs.	6	11	21	16	54
4. Cost-benefit analysis is being used primarily as a political weapon aimed at industry's favorite regulatory targets.	6	11	24	14	55
5. Cost-benefit analyses are usually biased to support the views of their sponsors.	11	6	30	7	54
6. Regulators implicitly place a value on life when they make decisions now, so they should be required to do so explicitly in the future.	11	6	17	21	55
7. Measuring costs and benefits precisely can be difficult, but such analyses are likely to improve environmental decisions.	16	1	29	9	55

#	Statement					
8.	Sound environmental policy requires greater analysis of costs and benefits to assure that scarce resources are wisely used.	15	2	31	7	55
9.	By acting only when benefits outweigh costs, regulators will simply be making public decisions in the same way individuals make private decisions.	5	12	6	32	55
10.	Analysis of costs and benefits should be encouraged, provided environmental regulators do not place too much emphasis on measuring impacts in dollars.	15	2	33	5	55
11.	It is unethical to place a dollar value on human life when making decisions involving the protection of human health.	4	13	28	10	55
12.	Analysis of costs and benefits should be encouraged so as to promote more cost-effective environmental regulations.	17	0	29	8	54
13.	Monetized cost-benefit analysis cannot contribute much to environmental decision making, because it depends on too many questionable assumptions and leaps of judgment.	4	13	24	14	55
14.	If the measurable costs of an environmental rule outweigh benefits, the rule should not be adopted.	3	13	1	36	53
15.	Regulators should not increase their efforts to measure in terms of dollars the costs and benefits of environmental rules.	1	16	10	27	54

*Note: Participants at Illinois Institute of Natural Resources and Conservation Foundation sponsored conference "Cost-Benefit Analysis in Environmental Regulation: Will It Clear the Air or Muddy the Water?" held in Chicago, October 15-16 1980. Total respondents equal 94. "Agree Strongly" and "Agree Slightly" reported as "Agree." "Disagree Strongly" and "Disagree Slightly" reported as "Disagree." Responses from participants identified as "Student," "Nonenvironmental government agency," "Academic," and "Other" not reported.

human life is unethical (statement 11).[7] Although the disagreement was not statistically significant on statement number 4, there was a visible trend toward disagreeing over whether cost-benefit analysis is primarily a political weapon.[8]

These answers indicate that there are still issues that must be resolved if we are to agree on whether or how to use cost-benefit analysis in environmental regulation. Of course, applying these survey results to the larger public policy debate is not without its limitations. In addition to the methodological problems mentioned earlier, there were some seemingly inconsistent responses. For instance, while everyone agreed that cost-benefit analysis should be encouraged, provided that dollars are not overemphasized (statement 10), participants also agreed, by implication, that efforts to measure in dollars the costs and benefits of environmental rules should continue (statement 15).

These inconsistencies may be solely a product of the questionnaire design, or they may represent actual ambivalence on the part of the participants. Regardless, they bolster, not detract from, the basic conclusions drawn from this informal study of attitudes. These conclusions are first, that much might be learned from doing a great deal more of this type of work among the participants in public policy making, and second, that efforts can be spent fruitfully on more clearly delineating agreements on the strengths and weaknesses of cost-benefit analysis and disagreements about which issues must be resolved in the methods, politics, and ethics of using cost-benefit analysis in environmental regulations.

The next three sections of this paper explore the strengths and limits of cost-benefit analysis and issues that must be resolved to achieve productive dialogue.

THE BENEFITS OF COST-BENEFIT ANALYSIS

Why was this group generally approving of cost-benefit analysis? It might have resulted from attending the conference. However, informal discussions after the event led us to conclude that people who favored cost-benefit analysis before attending the conference thought that the presentations were biased against cost-benefit analysis, while people who did not like cost-benefit analysis thought the speeches and discussions were too pro cost-benefit analysis. A show of hands at the beginning and at the end of the conference indicated that almost no one changed his or her mind.

The group's general approval of cost-benefit analysis might be attributed to the fact that cost-benefit analysis has much to commend it. First, cost-benefit analysis can help public decision makers make difficult resource allocations, given the reality of our finite world. Environmental and health protection are not our country's only legitimate social goals, and the resources do not exist to maximize health while completely reaching these other goals.[9] Cost-benefit analysis could provide a framework for deciding upon allocations. In these goal-setting tasks (what Andrews refers to as a "higher order of decisions"[10]) cost-benefit analysis could help us establish regulatory priorities, weed out least desirable alternatives, and increase the efficiency with which government attempts to maximize the total quality of life of its citizens.

Second, if used properly and carefully, cost-benefit analysis could display explicitly the rationale for decisions. This could elevate the level of public discussion and increase the usefulness of public participation in government decisions. "Although explicitness may increase controversy, it will also give greater focus and relevance to the debate, reducing the amount of uninformed or unconstructive rhetoric."[11]

Third, such an open and elevated inquiry could lead to better decisions, "better" defined as most efficient, most acceptable, or most wise. Decisions would likely be more informed if cost-benefit analysis provided more concise information and established useful limits upon the inquiry. More explicit decisions would be more accessible to the public, perhaps leading to more credibility in environmental regulatory programs.

Fourth, some argue that cost-benefit analysis would lead to more consistent regulations, thereby encouraging more efficient economic development. Regulatory decisions would likely be more cost-sensitive; this would further limit their marginal impact upon the U.S. economy.

Fifth, by highlighting the limits of data, cost-benefit analysis can indicate the extent of our ignorance and the levels of uncertainty involved in a decision. This would allow the public to evaluate the decision and point out areas for future research.

Sixth, by accumulating a catalog of cost-benefit analyses, policy makers could assess the cumulative positive and negative impacts of environmental regulations on selected populations or industries, on regions of the country, or on future generations. An historical perspective would be useful in analyzing decisions or groups of decisions over time.[12]

While cost-benefit analysis offers the above gains in environmental decision making, it is not without its problems. The next section will examine whether the use of cost-benefit analysis in agency decisions can be controlled to minimize these adverse impacts.

CONTROLLING ADVERSE IMPACTS

Even the most staunch advocates of cost-benefit analysis are willing to admit to some of its limitations. And critics offer a lengthy list of problems. While in theory the positive attributes of cost-benefit analysis are appealing, much of this appeal may be lost between abstraction and application.[13] Even the most beneficial of tools may do more harm than good if not used properly or circumspectly. From the literature reviewed in preparation for this book and from the practical experience reported in earlier chapters, we have compiled a checklist for those who are confronted by a cost-benefit analysis and wish to address its limitations.

Has the analyst carefully and correctly specified the policy question to be addressed? Check closely the analyst's statement of the problem. Has the action to be analyzed or that action's implications been misunderstood? Is the analysis consistent with basic economic theory (e.g., does it "analyze at the margins" or disallow "sunk costs")? Do the numbers overshadow a true understanding of the underlying impacts?

Most cost-benefit analyses reduce impacts to quantifiable figures to facilitate analysis. But some comprehension or "meaning" inevitably is lost in this reduction. Human lives can become tallymarks, days of suffering can become statistics, losses of livelihood can become mere figures. A common example of this is the frequent use of "damage coefficients," which purport to assign a dollar value of damage to each increment of pollution allowed. Saying that the conclusion is based upon a figure of one dollar per microgram per meter cubed per person per year can obscure the fact that this number is really just a surrogate for premature death, for the contraction of chronic illness, or for the irreplaceable loss of a scenic vista. In discussing Professor Weidenbaum's controversial conclusions on the costs of government's social programs, the House Subcommittee on Oversight and Government Operations noted that "the derivation and meaning of a figure is often lost in the public debate. The number is the thing."[14] So, too, in the midst of a cost-benefit analysis can we lose sight of the underlying impact when focusing too closely on aggregated numerical surrogates.[15]

Does the document overstep the quantity or quality of its data? Since all cost-benefit analyses are, to some extent, data-limited, it is important to view the analyst's conclusions in light of the amount or breadth of data available or the type of data collected. Statements about entire industries should not be based on data from only one point. Health statistics 10 years old may make poor bases for predictions 20 years hence.

Has the analyst directly addressed and explained the distributional impacts of the policy proposal? Does the analyst make any attempt to estimate or explain the distributional effects of the action being studied? Does the report describe or quantify the distribution of costs and benefits and how these distributions differ from one another? Neoclassical economics sometimes can identify the quantitative distribution of costs and benefits but cannot provide qualitative or normative statements about the results. Government action or environmental protection often must be based on these normative judgments. Is this conflict forthrightly addressed in the document and its implications for evaluating the conclusions explained? In addition, what discount rates were used and how were they justified?

It can be argued that in social policy decisions, discounting future benefits makes no logical sense, since no one is setting aside as an investment the money necessary to pay for future health or social impacts.[16] This is a particularly strong argument when dealing with intergenerational measurements.[17] Any use of discount rates for costs or benefits should be measured against the logic of actually discounting the events in question. For instance, future cash outlays traditionally are discounted, but why is a future premature death valued differently than one experienced today? Even when discounting appears logical, the rate established should be justified by the analyst, since this single choice can alter drastically and/or reverse the conclusions of the report.

Has the analyst overcome the too easily accepted bias toward overpredicting costs and underpredicting benefits? Dollars are a convenient yardstick for measuring costs but a difficult device for measuring death and suffering. Therefore the choice of money as a measuring tool often biases an analysis.[18] Does the cost-benefit analysis address this squarely and strive to equalize the measurement or at least estimate how much the measurement is distorted? Or does the document only focus on efficiency-related changes (primarily costs)? Since efficiencies are expressed easily in microeconomic terms, they are identified readily and may assume a disproportionate position in the analysis. Economists and engineers, the likely preparers of the cost-benefit analysis, are comfortable with cost analysis. Are benefits short-changed or simply stated as unmeasurable? If the same assumptions are not used to measure costs and benefits, are adequate reasons offered for different assumptions? When and how has the document placed a dollar value on things not normally subject to the marketplace? Monetizing nonmarket goods raises serious ethical questions. It also may jeopardize the credibility of the work in the eyes of the general public. Some decision makers with experience in using economic impact statements say that this practice is not necessary.[19] The methods for monetizing nonmarket goods are in their infancy, and the question whether such measurements can ever be validly and reliably made is still to be resolved.

Has the analyst used state-of-the-art techniques? For instance, what methods were used to forecast future circumstances? Straight-line, historically-based forecasts will hide the possibility of innovation or learning curves (which show achievement of efficiencies, through the gaining of experience). For example, the cost per kilowatt-hour of installing and operating a scrubber on an electrical generating plant may decrease as the industry gains experience. Projecting future costs as a function of our experience in the first few years of using this technology would not capture this adequately. To assume significant changes in near-term scenarios, however, adds an enormous element of subjectivity or just plain guesswork. And long-term projections should be *ipso facto* suspect in our rapidly changing world.

Is the document consistent with past work; if not, does it justify inconsistencies? If we begin conducting cost-benefit analyses on all major environmental regulatory proposals, we will quickly build a catalog of calculations, estimates, and analytical techniques. This should be used to aid both the analyst and the reviewer of the analysis. Past work should be included in the cost-benefit analysis. When past work is relied upon, however, its critical elements should be explained, not merely referenced. When the preparer rejects prior analyses, this also must be explicitly justified.

What is the impact of the judgments and assumptions made by the analyst? Are these judgments and assumptions valid? All of the conclusions of a cost-benefit analysis are more or less sensitive to the analyst's decisions in this area. Does the document provide a sensitivity analysis that would allow the decision maker, merely from reading the document, to understand how the quality, direction, and/or magnitude of the estimates might vary given different assumptions or judgments? Similarly, does the report highlight areas of uncertainty and estimate the magnitude of their impact? Even in the most clear cut of environmental health decisions uncertainty is epidemic. A cost-benefit analysis should take pains to highlight this. It should attempt to educate the decision maker as to the magnitude of the uncertainty and its effect upon the document's conclusions. Given the breadth and depth of uncertainties, a quality cost-benefit analysis will likely sound very tentative in its estimates of cost and benefits. A shoddy one may attach more firmness to its conclusions than is warranted. Which conclusions directly or indirectly result from hidden or implicit judgments and assumptions? Reviewing a cost-benefit analysis is a bit like playing detective. The logic of the analysis must be traced and fact must be separated from assumption, proof from judgment. Often assumptions are hidden inadvertently or are made unknowingly by a careless preparer. Since the analysis is never better than its assumptions, these hidden assumptions must be clarified and questioned along with those the analyst recognized and identified.

Is there evidence of bias in the document? Who prepared the cost-benefit analysis? Despite protests by some economists to the contrary, preparing a cost-benefit analysis is not an objective, value neutral exercise.[20] Experience has indicated that, in some cases, he or she who pays the piper calls the tune. A reviewer of a cost-benefit analysis should ask who prepared it, who paid for its preparation, and whose biases might have colored the analysis. A reviewer also should ask: "Does someone who might benefit from action based on the analysis have significant input to or control over the document?" This question may lead the reviewer to uncover a bias introduced by someone who stands to gain from the results of the analysis being skewed, magnified, or minimized. And where did the data come from? Many cost-benefit analyses are based wholly or in large part on data contributed by the industry or organization subject to the regulation being studied. All of the data in a cost-benefit analysis should be questioned and subjected to verification. As with any attempt to scrutinize the validity or reliability of any analysis (scientific, technological, or legal), information supplied by interested parties should be viewed skeptically and closely scrutinized.

How is cost-benefit analysis being used? The purpose of a cost-benefit analysis is to inform a decision maker. However, the results of many analyses find their way into the arguments and allegations of advocates. A cost-benefit analysis can provide a great deal of ammunition to someone's battle. The reviewer of an analysis should evaluate how much ammunition an analysis could provide and to whom. Is it being used in an honest attempt to educate or as propaganda masquerading as "objective" inquiry?

This checklist, lengthy as it is, would probably have to be doubled if cost-benefit analysis becomes commonplace in government decisions. More experience will likely reveal more limitations, even though some of the questions raised above may lose their importance as analysts improve their work. The relatively new profession of "public interest economist" will probably play a more significant role as environmentalists learn to cope with and, possibly, use to their advantage the analyses.

The checklist, numerous and weighty as it is, also shows that an educated and motivated advocate of environmental values has a number of "handles" available with which to minimize the adverse impacts of cost-benefit analysis. While a good cost-benefit analysis should bring forth its own limitations openly, honestly, and boldly, those that do not can be challenged, then verified or exposed. Should a productive dialogue lead to an increased use of cost-benefit analysis, participants can be assured that their creation can be bridled, although at a considerable expenditure of energy.

TO BE RESOLVED . . .

Even though cost-benefit analysis has some appealing virtues and seems subject to some control, it is highly unlikely that there will be a mad stampede of converted critics and born-again economists demonstrating vigorously for its inclusion in each and every environmental regulatory proposal. Many areas of disagreement still exist, and much needs to be resolved. Since at the time of this writing, the use of cost-benefit analysis is being "resolved" by recourse to the political battlefield, it is probably worthwhile to ask whether this controversy might be resolved better through a productive dialogue. The following, which will address this question, is divided into the resolution of methodological, political, and ethical issues.

Methods

The most basic question to be resolved is "what do we mean by cost-benefit analysis?" The term has been used to describe studies that are merely informal attempts to quantify the impacts of a proposal, studies that look at the economic impacts (primarily costs and macroeconomic effects) of regulations, and studies that are thorough, exhaustive examinations of all of the costs and benefits of a proposal. It is used as a simple descriptive term, as a politically charged rallying cry, and as invective. If productive dialogue is to help us reach some agreement on the use of cost-benefit analysis in environmental regulations, we will need to agree first on a common definition or set of definitions. This consensus may evolve from discussions or through examination of early attempts.[21]

We also will have to resolve when and how these analyses might be used. Should they be used on a case-by-case basis or to examine a portfolio of environmental regulations? Kevin Croke and Niels Herlevsen raise a series of programmatic design questions in an earlier paper which, being based upon their close analysis of Illinois' program over the last six years, should be given close attention. Cost-benefit analyses used as a priority-setting tool or as a screening process for judging which regulations deserve closer scrutiny probably would be more widely acceptable than those used to determine the exact level at which a regulation should establish a health- or welfare-related standard.

Because cost-benefit analyses are so extremely data-limited, it is difficult to imagine a program of vast application or substantial credibility that does not include a concerted effort to generate the important data on the linkages between source, discharge, pollution level, dose, health or welfare response, and economic impact. Establishing a catalog of cost-benefit analyses will aid this effort. Much could be learned, as well, from past regulatory decisions regarding the trading behavior between health and dollars that government decision makers exhibit. Of course, this "revealed preference" data should be viewed somewhat skeptically, since all of the economic, social, political, and ethical factors that affect a decision are not always evident from the regulation promulgated and an accompanying opinion.

Similar sophistication in state of the art analysis is needed to forecast both future trends in costs and macro effects and the likelihood and impact of innovation and learning curves. Without improving our work in these areas, cost-benefit analysis will be as credible as recent government anti-inflation programs that consistently demonstrate our inability to predict the future.

A standardized approach to discounting would be necessary for productive dialogue. What things should be discounted, over what relevant time periods, and at what rates? What are the implicit assumptions of discounting? When are they met, and when are they violated in environmental protection proposals?

If the opponents of cost-benefit analysis are going to lay down their swords, they will undoubtedly want all cost-benefit analyses to include healthy doses of sensitivity and uncertainty analyses. These may be no more complicated than a direct discussion of the limits of confidence that accompany the numbers in the analysis. For example: "we are 90% certain that the actual costs will lie between 5 million and 60 million dollars, with 30 million dollars as our best estimate." Cost-benefit analysis opponents more comfortable with quantified analysis might well desire a technical discussion of these problems, since the resulting numbers and graphs would likely indicate the enormous uncertainty and tenuousness of the conclusions made, particularly in the area of benefits.

It is an open question whether cost-benefit analysis actually contributes much to government decisions on health and safety problems. This is true partially because the goals of cost-benefit analysis are often not explicitly agreed upon, in part because there has been little experience to evaluate, but mostly because too few people have sought to do these evaluations, particularly over time. If cost-benefit analysis is worth conducting, it should be supported by rigorous and thorough program evaluations, not solely by reliance on *a priori* statements of its proponents. Our dialogue's discussants probably would wish some evidence of the benefits of cost-benefit analysis and the price we pay for its use. Unless we agree to do a cost-benefit analysis of cost-benefit analysis (through periodic review with a sunset provision), it is unlikely that its opponents will put aside their belief that cost-benefit analysis is merely a political weapon aimed at government programs that produce short-term costs for the private sector. Equally useful in dissipating this view might be the more widespread use of cost-benefit analysis in other government decisions, such as tobacco subsidies, weapons development, price supports, or import restrictions. If cost-benefit analysis is such an important tool for agency decision making, why is it not used in establishing priorities for massive budget cuts? Until this is answered satisfactorily, productive dialogue will be unlikely.

Proponents of cost-benefit analysis often admit the methodological difficulties mentioned elsewhere in this volume and above, but then proceed to argue that it still has its merits. Opponents say "come back when you've straightened out the bugs." In our dialogue, a heavy burden will rest on the former group to convince the latter that these problems are not fatal and that the adverse effects that might arise from the limits of such analyses can be controlled. Establishing a rigorous and aggressive nationwide peer review process might help if analysts are willing to criticize strongly shoddy or inferior work by their colleagues. Polite disagreement will not be sufficient. Opponents of cost-benefit analysis argue that it is an idea whose time has not come, methodologically speaking. They suspect the political motives of some of its proponents. A system to control, improve, and validate cost-benefit analysis will be needed, and dialogue will await such a proposal.

Politics
Political issues to be resolved arise from the use of cost-benefit analysis in decision making. Its opponents fear that poorly done analyses will be used, proving a disadvantage to environmental values. Productive dialogue will need to define clearly the enormous financial, labor, and time resources necessary for government to conduct worthwhile analyses and arrive at a guarantee that these resources will be committed.

Dialogue also must search for methods to limit the misuse and abuse of cost-benefit analysis. Decision makers will need to be educated as to how much or little they can expect from a cost-benefit analysis and with what cautions to view the results. All parties involved will have to fight strenuously the use of these results as propaganda or demagoguery both within and outside the policy-making process. It will be impossible to eliminate totally the use of cost-benefit analysis as a political weapon, but this practice must be discouraged or punished. Presentations of cost-benefit analysis in hearings should be made under oath and subject to full review and questioning by any interested party.

Just as environmental impact statements changed procedural aspects of government decision making, so too will cost-benefit analysis. Unless productive dialogue seeks and finds ways to accommodate these new tools into traditional, democratic, political decision making, the discussants will remain polarized. The clash between the positivistic notions of the analysis and the inherently relativistic nature of agency decisions will lead to difficulties. The analyst will frame the issues differently from the agency policy maker, may identify different points as relevant, and may be frustrated by opinions that appear to disregard or contradict the cost-benefit analysis. The decision maker will shy away from the bright explicitness brought to the decision by the cost-benefit analysis. Balancing nonquantified values with monetized results will prove difficult.

The literature contains a number of suggestions on how to accommodate cost-benefit analysis into traditional agency decision making. Our dialogue will have to consider using graded levels of cost considerations in enabling legislation,[22] shifting burdens of proof to give primacy to the nonquantifiable values,[23] and establishing strict or lenient standards of reviewability for the appellate courts to follow.[24]

The single most difficult political controversy to resolve will be the subject of citizen access and input into agency decisions that utilize cost-benefit analysis. As has been noted, a wide gap exists between the theoretical applicability of cost-benefit analysis and its actual use. Environmentalists are never going to be comfortable with cost-benefit analysis until they are assured that they have the access and ability to overcome the dangers of the gap between theory and practice.

Some have argued that, when properly done and used, CBA can open up agency decision making and allow significant public criticism of government actions. What this ignores is the problem of allowing public criticism of the analysis itself. As Richard N.L. Andrews notes earlier in this volume, the National Environmental Policy Act and Environmental Impact Statements enhanced the visibility of government decisions and encouraged input while cost-benefit analysis could provide a significant barrier to public participation.[25] The President's Commission on a National Agenda for the Eighties points out that public participation is critical if the country is going to make difficult resource allocation decisions that people will accept and follow.[26]

A fruitful discussion on cost-benefit analysis will have to spend much energy on ensuring that decisions using these analyses will be accessible to the public and to public interest groups. While government and the private sector have the resources and some expertise necessary to produce or analyze a cost-benefit analysis, public health and environmental groups lack both. They cannot develop their own data, construct their own cost-benefit analyses, or hire expensive experts to examine critically documents produced by others. Many environmentalists believe that this disparity is the most damaging aspect of proposals to use cost-benefit analysis in agency rulemaking. If the results of a cost-benefit analysis are ammunition, environmentalists argue that they do not have and cannot afford the guns with which to use these bullets. If environmentalists do not receive the resources to prepare their own documents and to critique the cost-benefit analyses prepared by government or industry, the controls mentioned earlier in this paper may not be very meaningful. If our dialogue tells the environmentalists that we recognize the limits of cost-benefit analysis but we are indifferent to their limited capability to control its use, we may not have a very productive dialogue. Such a "let them eat cake" attitude could destroy the credibility cost-benefit analysis might bring to government decisions and encourage continued polarization.

Ethics

At first glance the ethical arguments against cost-benefit analysis appear to be most difficult to resolve. But even here, productive dialogue might allow us to reach consensus and forestall factionalism. Current attempts to monetize nonmarket goods must be recognized as counter-intuitive. Economists must understand that methods to value prolonged life, such as discounted future earnings, which assign lower values to the lives of children and housewives, are not acceptable in a society that expects women and children to be saved first from a sinking ship. Cost-benefit proponents will have to admit to the dangers of reductionism pointed out by Steven Kelman, J.G.U. Adams, and others.[27] They will need to accept the fact that many of our government's decisions are based on a sense of duty or inherent rights and freely admit that their analyses can say little about such issues as the dignity of human life or the majesty of nature.[28]

On the other side, opponents of cost-benefit analysis must be willing to define the limits of ethical danger. Certainly some things are safely quantified and monetized while others are not. Which benefits of environmental regulations fall into the former and which into the latter category? Unless all of the participants in our discussion agree that there is a hierarchy of values assigned to environmental protection—that the more mundane benefits of pollution control or resource conservation can be assigned a dollar worth and that some higher orders of social values (such as the joys to a family of having long, healthy lives, or the awe humans sense on viewing nature's majesty) escape cost accounting—productive dialogue is impossible.

The second controversy that might be resolved through open and reasonable discussion focuses on conditions of uncertainty. All environmental decisions are fraught with uncertainty at many levels. In the late 1960s, our country made an implicit decision that we cared more to protect against underregulation than overregulation. Given uncertainty and risk, we chose to be given the benefit of the doubt in terms of health protection, even if this was inefficient from a cost standpoint. The 1970s saw a shifting away from that position, a swing of the pendulum toward protecting against overregulation. These positions were the result of political action, not rational discourse. The Commission on a National Agenda for the Eighties has asked for an explicit determination and clear direction to our agency decision makers as to "whether to err on the side of regulation, or to await more data when the evidence does not point clearly in one direction."[29] This will require categorizing the types of decisions faced (considering the types and amount of uncertainty and risk present) and clearly indicating when we err on the side of efficiency or when we protect ourselves, our health, and our environment from our own ignorance.

THE CHALLENGE

We have seen that it is possible to survey attitudes towards cost-benefit analysis. More of this must be done. We have seen that reasons for conducting cost-benefit analysis exist, and that its limitations can be controlled through careful examination of the document, through careful use of its results, and through a thoughtful structuring of the decision-making process in which the cost-benefit analysis is used. We have indicated areas in which dialogue must seek resolution in the methods, politics, and ethics of this practice. But why continue along this path? Why not choose up sides, hunker down, and prepare for political fistcuffs?

For one thing, we need a method for helping us make difficult decisions on where and how to allocate the scarce resources available to us in our finite world. Cost-benefit analysis, particularly if applied across all federal programs, might provide us with such a tool.

But we also cannot forget that environmental protection is not merely a budgetary standard or an accounting guideline. The logic of environmentalism is compelling, inescapable. The risks of not acting—premature death and the loss of our country's natural heritage—are irreversible. Preventing problems is not just good ecology; it is good economics and good ethics. No amount of anti-environmentalist or anti-government bravado will make the problems of living within a fragile biosphere go away. No amount of political rhetoric can reverse the basic laws of biology and physics.

If we sit back and take shots at one another, real progress in solving our economic and environmental problems will be impossible. We will continue experiencing a widely swinging political pendulum that will prove both inefficient and environmentally dangerous. In the long run, no one will win. We shall all lose.

Instead, we should strive to maximize agreement and search for methods to resolve remaining disagreements. This simple prescription for a constructive dialogue is often overlooked or ignored. Name-calling, posturing, histrionics, grandstanding are more than merely unprofessional. They will inevitably delay attainment of our health and environmental protection goals. Those who unthinkingly engage in these unproductive diatribes should be educated. Those who willfully pursue these tactics should be exposed.

Contention will be costly. After the current controversies die down and are replaced by other equally heated discussions, people will still be dying at too young an age and suffering will still be widespread, our natural heritage will still be in jeopardy of irretrievable loss, and the bald eagle, should it survive, will still be an important American asset to be preserved. The challenge of environmentalism in the 1980s is whether we can resolve the very controversies presented by the use of cost-benefit analysis. Can we learn to prosper in a finite world while dealing with the constraints presented by that basic reality? Can we engage in a productive dialogue which will move us forward toward that goal or will we engage in a political Armageddon while the time for action slowly slips away?

This book has attempted to review the work on cost-benefit analysis to date and enlighten the reader on the controversies surrounding the continuation or expansion of this practice. We hope it has succeeded in that.

But we also hope that it has illuminated a basic choice facing the participants in the making of environmental policy. We can fight or we can talk. We can be soldiers or we can be healers. The ultimate success of this effort rests with which path we take. The choice and the challenge remain.

Notes

1. Aside from the chapters in this volume, the reader may wish to consult A.M. Freeman, *The Benefits of Environmental Improvement: Theory and Practice* (Baltimore: Published for Resources for the Future by John Hopkins University Press, 1979); M.S. Baram, "Cost-Benefit Analysis: An Inadequate Basis for Health, Safety and Environmental Regulatory Decision-Making," *Ecology Law Quarterly* 8:473 (1980); W. Rodgers, "Benefits, Costs and Risks: Oversight of Health and Environmental Decision-Making," *Harvard Environmental Law Review* 4:191 (1980); "Cost-Benefit Analysis: Wonder Tool or Mirage," a report of the Subcommittee on Oversight and Investigations, House Committee on Interstate and Foreign Commerce (Committee Print 96—IFC 62, December 1980); and the symposium on this issue in *George Washington Law Review*, volume 45 (1977).

2. See Paul W. MacAvoy, "The E.P.A. Could Be Expendable," *The New York Times*, December 21, 1980; and Mark Green and Norman Waitzman, "Cost Analysis Needs Analyzing," *The New York Times*, February 8, 1980.

3. See George F. Will's column, "Value Fixing," *Washington Post*, January 18, 1981.

4. The total population was small ($N = 94$), and these people were a "survival group," since at least that many people had left the conference by the time the questionnaire was distributed. Those attending the conference hardly represented a cross-section of the general public—moreover, they had just finished listening to a day and a half of debate about cost-benefit analysis.

5. $X^2 = 13.146$, $p < 0.001$

6. $X^2 = 5.880$, $p < 0.025$

7. $X^2 = 10.170$, $p < 0.005$.

8. $X^2 = 2.64$, $p > 0.05$

9. J.C. Davies, S. Gusman, and Frances Irwin, "Determining Unreasonable Risk Under the Toxic Substances Control Act," (Washington, D.C.: The Conservation Foundation, 1981).

10. See Andrews' paper at page 130.

11. "Unreasonable Risk," at 6.

12. "Unreasonable Risk," at 10 and 18-19.

13. Numerous participants at the conference made this point without serious dispute from fellow panelists or from the audience. Also, see the Subcommittee report (*supra* note 1) at page 1, in which they say they found "strong indications that the actual use of cost-benefit analyses is even worse in practice than in theory." See also Andrews paper at page 119.

14. Subcommittee report at 10.

15. In the "Unreasonable Risk" report (*supra* note 9), the authors propose a nonmonetized, but still quantified measurement of health risks. Note, at pages 14-17, how this indicates the relative magnitude of the impacts of the alternatives but can obscure the fact that the difference amounts to the death of 20 people.

16. See F. Hapgood, "Risk-Benefit Analysis—Putting a Price on Life," *The Atlantic* 243:33 (January 1979).

17. As noted in Richard Liroff's earlier discussion of federal activity in this area, one case of poisoning today is worth 3 billion cases 450 years hence, using a 5% discount rate!

18. Douglas Costle compared this to judging the worth of a rendition of a Chopin etude by measuring the decibel level of the performance.

19. From personal conversations with Jacob Dumelle, Chairman of the Illinois Pollution Control Board, and Irvin Goodman, Vice-Chairman of the same agency.

20. In the *New York Times* article cited above (*supra* note 2), Green and Waitzman say that "given the consistent overstatement of costs and undervaluation of benefits, it is about as 'neutral' as literacy tests in the Old South."

21. A good start on this discussion can be found in Andrews' paper at pages 108-110.

22. See W. Rodgers, "Benefits, Costs and Risks: Oversight and Health and Environmental Decisionmaking," *Harvard Environmental Law Review* 4:191 (1980).

23. Ibid. and D. Doniger, "Federal Regulation of Vinyl Chloride: A Short Course in the Law and Policy of Toxic Substances Control," *Ecology Law Quarterly* 7:497 (1978).

24. Ibid. See also the report of the Subcommittee on Oversight and Investigations and the Minority Report accompanying it.

25. Andrews paper discusses this matter at page 124.

26. "A National Agenda for the Eighties," Report of the President's Commission, at page 95 (1980). Hereafter cited as "National Agenda."

27. See Kelman's paper earlier in this book. Also J.G.U.Adams, ". . . and How Much for Your Grandmother?" Environmental And Planning A 6:619 (1974); and L. Tribe, "Policy Science: Analysis or Ideology?" *Philosophy and Public Affairs* 2:66 (1979).

28. See Andrews' earlier paper for a discussion about economic optimality and normative constraints as differing bases for government action. Also see Kelman's paper in this volume.

29. "National Agenda" at 113.

Selected Bibliography on Cost-Benefit Analysis in Environmental Regulation

Ashford, Nicholas. "The Limits of Cost-Benefit Analysis in Regulatory Decisions" *Technology Review*, May 1980, p. 70.

Bailey, Martin J. *Reducing Risks to Life*. Washington, D.C.: American Enterprise Institute, 1980.

Baram, Michael S. "Cost-Benefit Analysis: An Inadequate Basis for Health, Safety, and Environmental Regulatory Decision-making." 8 *Ecology L.Q.* 473, 1980.

Ben-David, Shaul *et al.* "A Study of The Ethical Foundations of Benefit-Cost Analysis Techniques." Working Paper, Department of Economics, University of New Mexico, August 1979.

Bernick, Kathryne. "The Inflation Impact Statement Program and Executive Branch Coordination." Draft Report to American Bar Association, Commission on Law and the Economy. Washington, D.C.: May 1977.

Boulding, Kenneth. "The Ethics of Rational Decision." 12 *Management Sciences* B-161, 1966.

Clark, Timothy B. "How RARG has Regulated the Regulators." 11 *National Journal* 1700, October 13, 1979.

Clark, Timothy B. "The Costs and Benefits of Regulation — Who Knows How Great They Really Are?" 11 *National Journal 2023, December 1, 1979.*

"Comment: Assessing Regulatory Costs and Benefits: Fifth Circuit Vacates OSHA Benzene Standard." 8 *Environmental Law Reporter* 10250, 1978.

"Comment: Supreme Court's Divided *Benzene* Decision Preserves Uncertainty over Regulation of Carcinogens." 10 *Environmental Law Reporter* 10192,1980.

Connolly, Walter B., Jr. "Court's Benzene Decision Sheds Almost No Light." *Legal Times of Washington*. August 4, 1980, p. 14.

DeLong, James V. "*Benzene* Exposes Workers to Unresolved Issues." *Legal Times of Washington*. September 8, 1980, p. 40.

DeMuth, Christopher C. "The White House Review Programs." *Regulation*. January/February 1980, p. 13.

DeMuth, Christopher C. "The Regulatory Budget." *Regulation* March/April 1980, p. 29.

Davies, J. Clarence *et al.* "Determining Unreasonable Risk Under the Toxic Substances Control Act." Washington, D.C.: The Conservation Foundation, 1979.

Doniger, David D. *The Law and Policy of Toxic Substances Control: A Case Study of Vinyl Chloride.* Baltimore, MD: Johns Hopkins University Press for Resources for the Future, 1978.

Doniger, David D. "Defeat in Benzene Exposure Case No Death Knoll for OSHA Standards." *The National Law Journal.* September 15, 1980, p. 26.

Environmental Law Institute, Toxic Substances Program." Cost-Benefit Analysis and Environmental, Health and Safety Regulation: An Overview of the Agencies and Legislation." Washington, D.C.: February 1980.

Ferguson, Allen R. and E. Phillip LeVeen. *The Benefits of Health and Safety Regulation.* Cambridge, MA: Ballinger Publishing Company, 1981.

Fischhoff, Baruch. "Cost-Benefit Analysis and the Art of Motorcycle Maintenance." 8 *Policy Sciences* 177, 1977.

Freeman, A. Myrick. "The Benefits of Air and Water Pollution Control: A Review and Synthesis of Recent Estimates." Report prepared for U.S. Council on Environmental Quality, December 1979.

Gori, Gio Batta. "The Regulation of Carcinogenic Hazards." 208 *Science* 256, April 18, 1980.

Green, Harold P. "Cost-Risk Benefit Assessment and the Law — Introduction and Perspective." 45 *George Washington L. Rev.* 901, 1977.

Hapgood, Fred. "Risk-Benefit Analysis — Putting a Price on Life." *The Atlantic.* January 1979, p. 33.

"Has Environmental Regulation Gone Too Far? A Debate on the Costs versus the Benefits." *Chemical and Engineering News.* April 23, 1979, p. 25.

Junger, Peter D. "The Inapplicability of Cost-Benefit Analysis to Environmental Policies." 46 *Ekistics* 184, May/June 1979.

Kasper, Raphael. "Cost-Benefit Analysis in Environmental Decision-Making." 45 *George Washington L. Rev.* 1013, 1977.

Kosters, Marvin. "Counting the Costs." *Regulation*, July/August 1979, p. 17.

Leape, James P. "Quantitative Risk Assessment in Regulation of Environmental Carcinogens." 4 *Harvard Environmental L. Rev.* 86., 1980.

Lovins, Amory. "Cost-Risk Benefit Assessments in Energy Policy." 45 *George Washington L. Rev.* 911, 1977.

Mendeloff, John. "Reducing Occupational Health Risks:, Uncertain Effects and Unstated Benefits." *Technology Review*, May 1980, p. 67.

Merrill, Richard D. "Risk-Benefit Decisionmaking by the Food and Drug Administration." 45 *George Washington L. Rev.* 994, 1977.

National Academy of Sciences, Committee on Environmental Decision-Making. "Decision-Making in the Environmental Protection Agency — Volume II." Washington, D.C., 1977.

National Commission on Air Quality. "Report to the National Commission on Air Quality of the Benefit Methodology Evaluation Panel." Washington, D.C., May 1980.

Okrent, David. "Comment on Societal Risk." 208 *Science* 372, April 25, 1980.

Putnum, Hayes, and Bartlett, Inc. "Comparisons of Estimated and Actual Pollution Control Costs for Selected Industries." Report prepared for U.S. EPA Office of Planning and Evaluation, February 1980.

Reich, Robert B. "Warring Critiques of Regulation." *Regulation*, February 1979, p. 37.

Rhoads, Steven E. "How Much Should We Spend to Save A Life?" *The Public Interest*, Spring 1978, p. 74.

Rodgers, William H. Jr. "Benefits, Costs, and Risks: Oversight of Health and Environmental Decisionmaking." 4 *Harvard Environmental L. Rev.* 191,1980.

Rowe, William D. "Governmental Regulation of Societal Risks." 45 *George Washington L. Rev.* 944, 1977.

Singer, Max. "How to Reduce Risks Rationally." *The Public Interest*, Spring 1978, p. 93.

Smith, R. Jeffrey. "A Light Rein Falls on OSHA." 209 *Science* 567, August 1,1980.

Starr, Chauncey and Chris Whipple. "Risks of Risk Decisions." 208 *Science* 1114, June 6, 1980.

Tolchin, Susan. "Presidential Power and the Politics of RARG." *Regulation*, July/August 1979, p. 44.

Tribe, Lawrence H. "Ways Not to Think About Plastic Trees." 83 *Yale L. J.* 1315, 1974.

Tribe, Lawrence H. "Policy Science: Analysis or Ideology?" 2 *Philosophy and Public Affairs* 66, 1979.

U.S. Congress. House Committee on Interstate and Foreign Commerce, Subcommittee on Oversight and Investigations. "Cost-Benefit Analysis: Wonder Tool or Mirage?" 96th Cong., 2d Sess., December 1980, Comm. Print 96-1FC62.

U.S. Congress. House Committee on Interstate and Foreign Commerce, Subcommittee on Oversight and Investigations. "Federal Regulation and Regulatory Reform." 94th Cong., 2d Sess., October 1976, H. Doc. No. 95-134.

U.S. Congress. House Committee on Interstate and Foreign Commerce. "Use of Cost-Benefit Analysis by Regulatory Agencies." 96th Cong., 1st Sess., 1979, Serial No. 96-157.

U.S. Congress. House Committee on Science and Technology and Committee on Commerce, Science and Transportation. "Risk-Benefit Analysis in the Legislative Process." 96th Cong., 1st Sess., 1980. Serial KK.

U.S. Congress. Joint Economic Committee. "Regulatory Budgeting and the Need for Cost-Effectiveness in the Regulatory Process." 96th Cong., 1st. Sess., 1979.

U.S. Congress. Senate Committee on Environment and Public Works, Subcommittee on Environmental Pollution. "Executive Branch Review of Environmental Regulations." 96th Cong., 1st Sess., 1979. Serial No. 96-H4.

U.S. Congress. Senate Committee on Environment and Public Works. "The Status of Environmental Economics: An Update." Report prepared by the Environmental and Natural Resources Policy Division, Congressional Research Service, Library of Congress. 96th Cong., 1st Sess., July 1979. Serial No. 96-6.

U.S. Congress. Senate Committee on Governmental Affairs. "The Benefits of Environmental, Health, and Safety Regulation." Report prepared by Nicholas A. Ashford *et al.*, M.I.T. Center for Policy Alternatives. 96th Cong., 2d Sess., 1980.

U.S. Council on Environmental Quality. "Environmental Quality — 1979." Washington, D.C.: Government Printing Office, 1979.

U.S. Environmental Protection Agency Science Advisory Board, Subcommittee on Economic Analysis. "Economics in EPA." Washington, D.C., June 1980.

U.S. Regulatory Council. "A Survey of Ten Agencies' Experience With Regulatory Analysis." Washington, D.C., 1981.

Weaver, Suzanne. "Inhaber and the Limits of Cost-Benefit Analysis." *Regulation*, July/August 1979, p. 14.

Wildavsky, Aaron. *The Politics of the Budgetary Process.* Boston: Little, Brown & Co., 2d ed., 1974.

Williams, Deborah Lee. "Benefit-Cost Assessment in Natural Resources Decision-making: An Economic and Legal Overview." 11 *Natural Resources Lawyer* 761, 1979.

The Authors

Richard N. L. Andrews is the Director of the Institute for Environmental Studies at the University of North Carolina. Previously, he was Associate Professor and Chairman of the Natural Resource Policy and Management Program University of Michigan. Dr. Andrews is the author of *Environmental Policy and Administrative Change* (Lexington, 1976) and coauthor of *Environmental Values in Public Decisions: A Research Agenda* (1978). He has published numerous articles on environmental policy and administrative planning. Dr. Andrews received a B.A. in Philosophy from Yale University, and a Master's in Regional planning and a Ph.D. in City and Regional Planning from the University of North Carolina.

Kevin G. Croke, an Associate Professor in the Health Resources Management Program, University of Illinois School of Public Health since 1974, has taught courses in environmental policy, transportation planning, and health program management. He has been a consultant on numerous environmental and energy projects, including an Illinois Institute for Environmental Quality effort to evaluate the cost and effectiveness of alternative carbon monoxide control plans for Chicago. He is coauthor of *Urban Transportation and the Environment* (1974). His papers have been published in the *Journal of the Air Pollution Control Association* and in many conference proceedings. Dr. Croke received B.S. and Ph.D. degrees from Northwestern University.

Robert G. Fabian is a Research Assistant in Economics at the University of Chicago. His major research interest is the application of cost-benefit analysis to environmental regulations. In addition, he has collaborated on reports and articles about air, water, and noise pollution and currently is participating in a visibility valuation project at the University of Chicago. Mr. Fabian has a B.A. in Economics from the University of Notre Dame, an M.A. in Economics from the University of Illinois, and a Ph.D. in Economics from the University of Florida.

Niels B. Herlevsen manages the Economic Analysis Program at the Illinois Institute of Natural Resources, an agency that, through research in information activities, promotes wise and balanced use of Illinois' natural resources. Mr. Herlevsen's current area of expertise is the application of environmental economics to natural resources and development in the state of Illinois. Mr. Herlevsen has contributed to a book on the emergence and development of the global economy. He received a B.A. in Economics from Northwestern University and is a member of the Environment and Natural Resource Economists Association.

Arthur P. Hurter, Jr. has been Chairman of the Department of Industrial Engineering and Management Sciences at Northwestern University since 1969.

Among his numerous current interests are capital budgeting, investment planning, project selection and evaluation, plant and activity location, cost-benefit analysis, and urban land-use planning. Dr. Hurter has published extensively on these and other engineering and management matters. He has earned B.S. and M.S. degrees in Chemical Engineering and M.A. and Ph.D. degrees in Economics, all from Northwestern University.

Steven Kelman, Assistant Professor of Public Policy at the Kennedy School of Government at Harvard University, is on leave for 1980-81 to serve as Associate Director for Management Planning, Bureau of Consumer Protection, Federal Trade Commission. Dr. Kelman has written extensively in the field of health and safety regulation; his book, *Regulating America, Regulating Sweden: A Comparative Study of Occupational Safety and Health Policies,* was published in December 1980 by the MIT Press. A graduate of Harvard College, Dr. Kelman received his Ph.D. in Government from Harvard University.

Richard A. Liroff is a Senior Associate at The Conservation Foundation. He is the author of *A National Policy for the Environment: NEPA and Its Aftermath* (Indiana University Press, 1976), and coauthor of *Protecting Open Space: Land Use Control in the Adirondack Park* (Ballinger Publishing Company, 1981). He is also the author of The Conservation Foundation Issue Report, *Air Pollution Offsets: Trading, Selling, and Banking* (1980). Liroff received his Ph.D. in Political Science from Northwestern University and a B.A. in Politics from Brandeis University.

Daniel Swartzman has been Assistant Professor of Health Resources Management at the University of Illinois School of Public Health since 1978, teaching courses in public health advocacy, policy analysis, environmental law, and public decision making. From 1975 to 1979, he was Director of Legal Services for the Chicago Lung Association. He has served on numerous committees and boards, including the Environmental Law Committee and the Legislative Committee of the Chicago Bar Association; the Section Council of the Environmental Control Law Section of the Illinois State Bar Association; the National Air Conservation Commission; the Executive Board of the Illinois Environmental Council; the Board of Directors of the National Clean Air Coalition; and the Illinois Institute of Natural Resources Economic Technical Advisory Committee (as public health representative). Mr. Swartzman received a B.A. from the University of Washington, a J.D. from Northwestern University School of Law, and a Master's in Public Health from the University of Illinois School of Public Health.

George S. Tolley, Professor of Economics at the University of Chicago since 1966, also serves as Director of the University's Center for Urban Studies. From 1974 to 1975, he was Deputy Assistant Secretary and Director of the Office of Tax Analysis, U.S. Department of the Treasury; and from 1965 to 1966 he was Director of the Economic Development Division, Economic Research Service, U.S. Department of Agriculture. He has served on numerous national and international committees, task forces, and editorial boards. The author of several books, primarily dealing with agricultural or urban economics, Dr. Tolley has published extensively in journals, technical publications, and conference proceedings. A graduate of American University, he received a Ph.D. in Economics from the University of Chicago.